Bed & Breakfast Stops

2011

in Britain

- **For Holidaymakers and Business Travellers**
- **Overnight Stops and Short Breaks**

Panda Villa, Edinburgh, (page 314)

ISBN 978-1-85055-436-3

Typeset by FHG Guides Ltd, Paisley.
Printed and bound in China by Imago.

Distribution. Book Trade: ORCA Book Services, Stanley House,
3 Fleets Lane, Poole, Dorset BH15 3AJ
(Tel: 01202 665432; Fax: 01202 666219)
e-mail: mail@orcabookservices.co.uk
Published by FHG Guides Ltd., Abbey Mill Business Centre,
Seedhill, Paisley PA1 ITJ (Tel: 0141-887 0428 Fax: 0141-889 7204).
e-mail: admin@fhguides.co.uk

Bed & Breakfast Stops in Britain is published by FHG Guides Ltd,
part of Kuperard Group.

Cover design: FHG Guides
Cover Picture: with thanks to Buckle Yeat Guest House, Near Sawrey, Cumbria (page 268)

symbols

	Totally non-smoking		Pets Welcome
	Children Welcome		Short Breaks
	Suitable for Disabled Guests		Licensed

Contents

©MAPS IN MINUTES™ / Collins Bartholomew (2009)

Looking for Holiday Accommodation?
then visit our website:
www.holidayguides.com

**Search for holiday accommodation
by region, location, type of accommodation
(B&B, Self-Catering, Hotel etc)**

**Special requirements –
Are you looking for accommodation
where children and pets are welcome
or maybe you want to be
close to a golf course...**

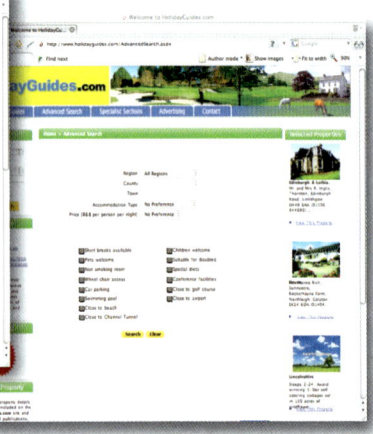

for details of hundreds of properties throughout the UK

Accommodation Standards: Star Grading Scheme

The AA, VisitBritain, VisitScotland, and the VisitWales now use a single method of assessing and rating serviced accommodation. Irrespective of which organisation inspects an establishment the rating awarded will be the same, using a common set of standards, giving a clear guide of what to expect. They have full details of the grading system on their websites.

www.enjoyEngland.com

Scottish www.visitScotland.com

 www.visitWales.com

www.theaa.com

Using a scale of 1-5 stars the objective quality ratings give a clear indication of accommodation standard, cleanliness, ambience, hospitality, service and food.

This shows the full range of standards suitable for every budget and preference, and allows visitors to distinguish between the quality of accommodation and facilities on offer in different establishments. All types of board and self-catering accommodation are covered, including hotels, B&Bs, holiday parks, campus accommodation, hostels, caravans and camping, and boats.

Gold and Silver awards are given to Hotels and Guest Accommodation that provide exceptional quality, especially in service and hospitality.

The more stars, the higher level of quality

★
acceptable quality; simple, practical, no frills

★★
good quality, well presented and well run

★★★
very good level of quality and comfort

★★★★
excellent standard throughout

★★★★★
exceptional quality, with a degree of luxury

National Accessible Scheme Logos for mobility impaired and older people

If you have particular mobility impairment. look out for the National Accessible Scheme. You can be confident of finding accommodation or attractions that meet your needs by looking for the following symbols.

 Older and less mobile guests
If you have sufficient mobility to climb a flight of steps but would benefit from fixtures and fittings to aid balance.

 Part-time wheelchair users
You have restricted walking ability or may need to use a wheelchair some of the time and can negotiate a maximum of 3 steps.

 Independent wheelchair users
You are a wheelchair user and travel independently. Similar to the international logo for independent wheelchair users.

 Assisted wheelchair users
You're a wheelchair user and travel with a friend or family member who helps you with everyday tasks.

England and Wales • Counties

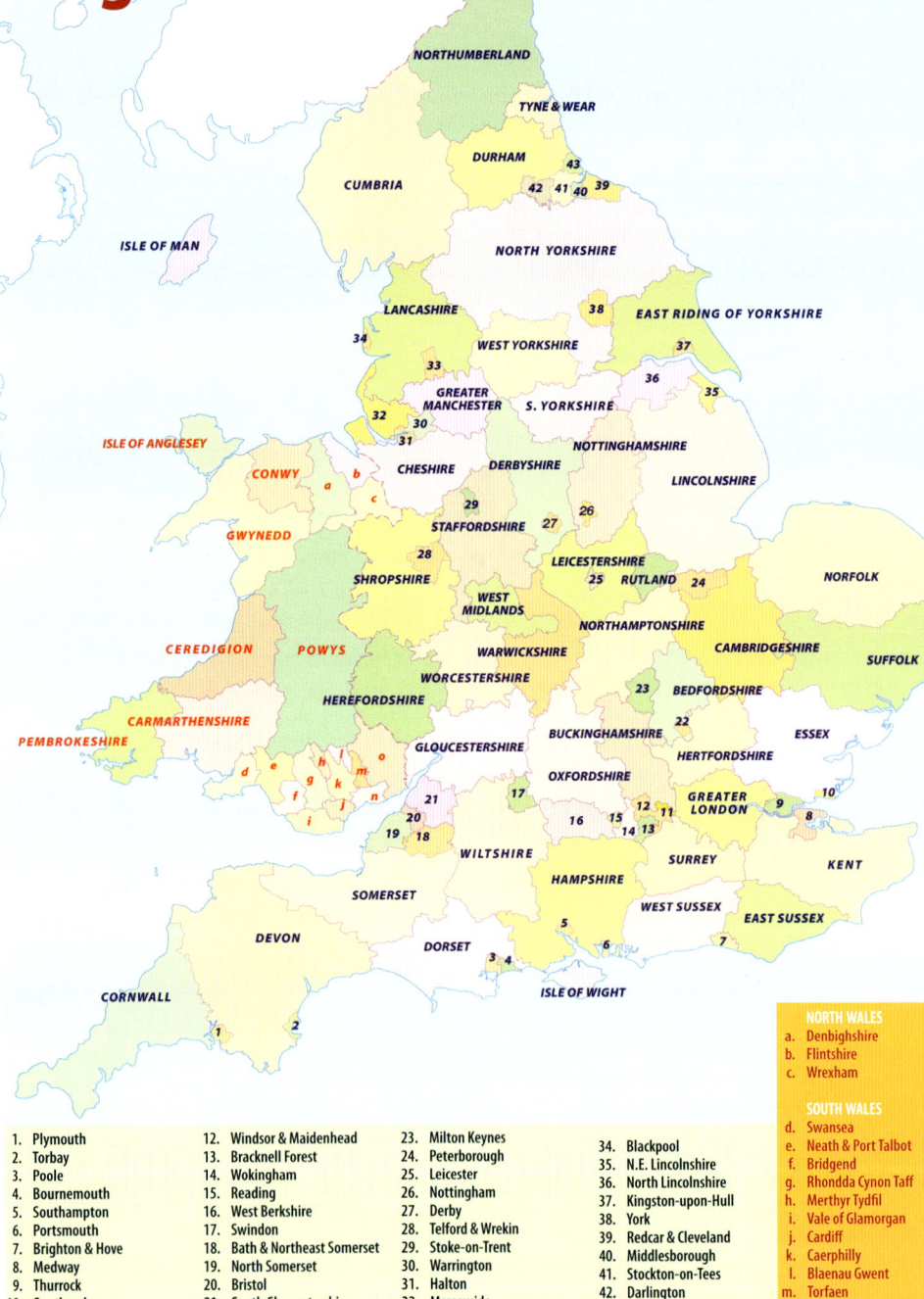

NORTHUMBERLAND

TYNE & WEAR

DURHAM

43

CUMBRIA

42 41 40 39

ISLE OF MAN

NORTH YORKSHIRE

LANCASHIRE

38

EAST RIDING OF YORKSHIRE

34

WEST YORKSHIRE

37

33

36

GREATER MANCHESTER

35

32

30

S. YORKSHIRE

ISLE OF ANGLESEY

31

CONWY

a

b

CHESHIRE

DERBYSHIRE

NOTTINGHAMSHIRE

c

LINCOLNSHIRE

GWYNEDD

29

STAFFORDSHIRE

26

27

28

LEICESTERSHIRE

NORFOLK

SHROPSHIRE

WEST MIDLANDS

25

RUTLAND

24

CEREDIGION

POWYS

WARWICKSHIRE

NORTHAMPTONSHIRE

CAMBRIDGESHIRE

SUFFOLK

WORCESTERSHIRE

23

BEDFORDSHIRE

CARMARTHENSHIRE

HEREFORDSHIRE

22

ESSEX

PEMBROKESHIRE

d e

h

l m o

BUCKINGHAMSHIRE

HERTFORDSHIRE

f g

k n

GLOUCESTERSHIRE

OXFORDSHIRE

GREATER LONDON

9

10

i

21

17

12

11

8

20

16

15

14 13

SURREY

KENT

19

18

WILTSHIRE

SOMERSET

HAMPSHIRE

WEST SUSSEX

EAST SUSSEX

DEVON

DORSET

5

3 4

6

7

CORNWALL

ISLE OF WIGHT

1

2

1. Plymouth	12. Windsor & Maidenhead	23. Milton Keynes	34. Blackpool	**NORTH WALES**
2. Torbay	13. Bracknell Forest	24. Peterborough	35. N.E. Lincolnshire	a. Denbighshire
3. Poole	14. Wokingham	25. Leicester	36. North Lincolnshire	b. Flintshire
4. Bournemouth	15. Reading	26. Nottingham	37. Kingston-upon-Hull	c. Wrexham
5. Southampton	16. West Berkshire	27. Derby	38. York	
6. Portsmouth	17. Swindon	28. Telford & Wrekin	39. Redcar & Cleveland	**SOUTH WALES**
7. Brighton & Hove	18. Bath & Northeast Somerset	29. Stoke-on-Trent	40. Middlesborough	d. Swansea
8. Medway	19. North Somerset	30. Warrington	41. Stockton-on-Tees	e. Neath & Port Talbot
9. Thurrock	20. Bristol	31. Halton	42. Darlington	f. Bridgend
10. Southend	21. South Gloucestershire	32. Merseyside	43. Hartlepool	g. Rhondda Cynon Taff
11. Slough	22. Luton	33. Blackburn with Darwen		h. Merthyr Tydfil
				i. Vale of Glamorgan
				j. Cardiff
				k. Caerphilly
				l. Blaenau Gwent
				m. Torfaen
				n. Newport
				o. Monmouthshire

Cornwall

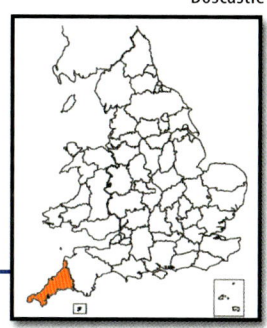

Cornwall, with the longest stretch of coastline in the UK, has become a major centre for watersports, whether sailing, surfing, windsurfing, water-skiing, diving in the clear waters to explore historic wrecks or enjoying a family beach holiday. There are busy fishing towns like Looe, Padstow, and traditional villages such as Polperro, with plenty of inns and restaurants where you can sample the fresh catch. There are gardens at Mount Edgcumbe and the Lost Garden of Heligan, as well as a wide choice of National Trust properties including Lanhydrock. The magnificent coast is ideal for birdwatchers, artists and photographers, while Bodmin Moor, one of Cornwall's 12 Areas of Outstanding Natural Beauty, is well worth a visit.

Callington, Crantock, Falmouth

Fowey, Helston

The Old Ferry Inn

Why not come for a well deserved holiday to the family-run Old Ferry Inn, close to the edge of the beautiful River Fowey. There are many varied walks from country and riverside to breathtaking views along the Cornwall Coastal Path. The 400-year-old hotel has an excellent à la carte restaurant for evening meals and a comprehensive bar menu for lunch and evening. The Inn has 12 letting rooms with tea and coffee making facilities, colour TV and telephone. All rooms have en suite or private facilities, and most have river views.

Prices are from £90-£130 per night for two people sharing.

Bodinnick-by-Fowey PL23 1LX
Tel: (01726) 870237 • Fax: (01726) 870116
www.oldferryinn.com • e-mail: royce972@aol.com

Hendra Farm, just off the main Helston/Falmouth road, is an ideal centre for touring Cornwall; three miles to Helston, eight to both Redruth and Falmouth. Safe sandy beaches within easy reach – five miles to the sea.

Two double, one single, and one family bedrooms with washbasins and tea-making facilities; bathroom and toilets; sittingroom and two diningrooms.

• Cot, babysitting and reduced rates offered for children.
• No objection to pets • Car necessary, parking space.
• Open all year except Christmas • Evening Dinner optional • Tea and homemade cake before bed.
Bed and Breakfast only from £20 per night.

Mrs P. Roberts, Hendra Farm, Wendron, Helston TR13 0NR (01326 340470)

SB

symbols

   Totally non-smoking   Pets Welcome

   Children Welcome   **SB** Short Breaks available

   Suitable for Disabled Guests Licensed

Colliford Tavern   "AN OASIS ON BODMIN MOOR"

Colliford Lake, Near St Neot, Liskeard, Cornwall PL14 6PZ • Tel: 01208 821335
e-mail: info@colliford.com • www.colliford.com

SB

Set in attractive grounds which include a children's play area, ponds and a working waterwheel, this delightfully furnished free house offers good food and bar snacks. Sprucely-appointed guest rooms are spacious and have en suite shower, colour television, radio alarm, beverage maker and numerous thoughtful extras.

An unusual feature of the tavern is a 37' deep granite well. In the midst of the scenic splendour of Bodmin Moor, this is a relaxing country retreat only a few minutes' walk from Colliford Lake, so popular with fly fishermen. Both north and south coasts are within easy driving distance and terms are most reasonable.

enjoyEngland.com
★★★★
INN

Campsite for touring caravans, motorhomes and tents - full electric hook-up etc available.

Gallen-Treath
GUEST HOUSE

AA
★★★
Guest House

SB

PORTHALLOW,
ST KEVERNE, HELSTON,
CORNWALL TR12 6PL
Tel & Fax: 01326 280400

Friendly guesthouse with spectacular coastal views, comfortable en suite rooms, hearty meals and a warm welcome. Close to coastal path, diving, gardens and more. Traditional breakfasts.

e-mail: gallentreath@btclick.com

www.gallen-treath.com

Bay View Farm

"Enjoy our little piece of paradise"

In a spectacular location, enjoying uninterrupted views of Looe and St George's Island, our coastal farm is a haven for the walker and birdwatcher – you can meet our Shire horses too. This beautifully decorated and furnished bungalow has three spacious en suite bedrooms, two with their own large conservatory with lovely valley views. They offer every comfort, including colour TV, central heating and beverage trays. There is ample parking, and wheelchair access if required. Savour delicious meals whilst gazing across the water, relax in the lounge or on the patio and watch the sun setting over Looe.

SB

- Exceptional location
- Luxury rooms with sea or rural view
- 10 minute walk down to the South West Coastal Path to Millendreath Beach
- Prize-winning Shire Horses
- Ample parking
- Wheelchair-friendly
- No Smoking

Looe, Lostwithiel, Mawgan Porth

SB

SB

Newquay

Padstow, Penzance

SB

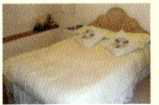

Bolankan Cottage B&B

Crows-an-Wra, St Buryan, Penzance TR19 6HU

Lynn & Les Cox • Tel: 01736 810168

Bolankancottage@talktalk.net • www.bolankan-cottage.co.uk

Fully modernised B&B approximately halfway between
Penzance and Land's End.

Double, twin and family rooms all en suite with central
heating, colour TV, hairdryer and tea/coffee making facilities.
Off-road parking.

B&B from £55 per room based on 2 sharing

Mrs P. White, Seaways, Polzeath PL27 6SU
Tel: 01208 862382
e-mail: pauline@seaways99.freeserve.co.uk
www.seawaysguesthouse.co.uk

Seaways is a small family guest house, 250 yards from safe, sandy beach. Surfing, riding, sailing, tennis, squash, golf all nearby. All bedrooms with en suite or private bathrooms, comprising one family, two double, two twin and a single room. Sittingroom; dining room. Children welcome (reduced price for under 10s). Cot, high chair available. Comfortable family holiday assured with plenty of good home cooking. Lovely cliff walks nearby. Padstow a short distance by ferry. Other places of interest include Tintagel, Boscastle and Port Isaac.

Non-smoking establishment.
Open all year round.
Bed and Breakfast £38pppn.

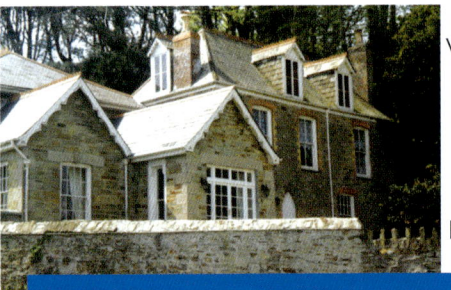

St Austell

SB

**Mrs Dawn Rundle, Lancallan Farm,
Mevagissey, St Austell PL26 6EW
Tel & Fax: 01726 842284
e-mail: dawn@lancallan.fsnet.co.uk
www.lancallanfarm.co.uk**

Lancallan is a large 17th century farmhouse on a working 700-acre dairy and beef farm in a beautiful rural setting, one mile from Mevagissey. We are close to Heligan Gardens, lovely coastal walks and sandy beaches, and are well situated for day trips throughout Cornwall. Also six to eight miles from the Eden Project (20 minutes' drive). Enjoy a traditional farmhouse breakfast in a warm and friendly atmosphere.

The farmhouse comprises three bedrooms to let, two are double en suite and the third is a family room with one double and one single bed with a private bathroom. All bedrooms have a colour TV, tea and coffee making facilities, a hairdryer, towels and toiletries. There is a separate dining room for guests, and a relaxing lounge.

Terms and brochure available on request. SAE please.

SB

Polgreen is a family-run dairy farm nestling in the Pentewan Valley in an Area of Outstanding Natural Beauty. One mile from the coast and four miles from the picturesque fishing village of Mevagissey, a perfect location for a relaxing holiday in the

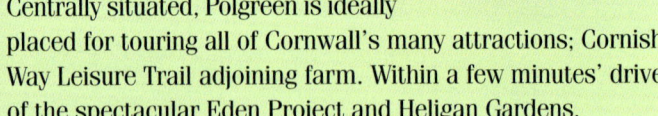

glorious Cornish countryside. Centrally situated, Polgreen is ideally

placed for touring all of Cornwall's many attractions; Cornish Way Leisure Trail adjoining farm. Within a few minutes' drive of the spectacular Eden Project and Heligan Gardens.
All rooms with private facilities, colour TV, tea/coffee making facilities. Guest lounge. Children welcome.
Terms from £30 per person per night.

**Mrs Liz Berryman, Polgreen Farm, London Apprentice,
St Austell PL26 7AP • Tel: 01726 75151
e-mail: polgreen.farm@btinternet.com
www.polgreenfarm.co.uk**

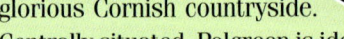

AA
★★★★
Guest
Accommodation

St Mawgan, Truro

Please note...

All the information in this book is given in good faith in the belief that it is correct. However, the publishers cannot guarantee the facts given in these pages, neither are they responsible for changes in policy, ownership or terms that may take place after the date of going to press. Readers should always satisfy themselves that the facilities they require are available and that the terms, if quoted, still apply.

Devon

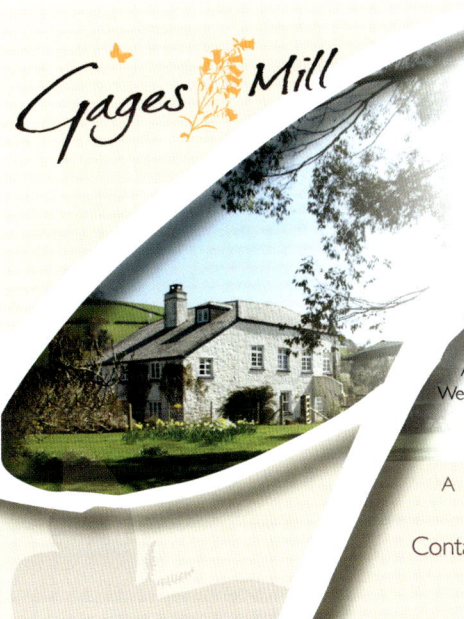

Gages Mill, a Grade 2 listed former fulling mill, is set in over an acre of beautiful grounds on the edge of Dartmoor National Park.

Six double and one (ground floor) twin room. All rooms furnished to a high standard with tea and coffee making facilities, hairdryer and radio alarm clock. Free parking on site.

Breakfast is all or any of full English breakfast (locally sourced where possible), cereals, fruits, teas, filtered coffee and juices.

Families with children welcome •
A few minutes walk from the centre of Ashburton •
We are licensed to sell a selection of beers and wines •

COUNTRY GUEST HOUSE

A S H B U R T O N   D E V O N

Contact Kate or Nathan on 01364 652391
or email: katestone@gagesmill.co.uk

www.gagesmill.co.uk

Think of moorland, and Devon immediately comes to mind. A county of contrasts, to the north are the wild moors of the Exmoor National Park, fringed by dramatic cliffs and combes, golden beaches and picturesque harbours, with busy market towns and sleepy villages near the coast. For family holidays, one of the best known of the many Blue Flag beaches on the north coast is at Woolacombe, with three miles of sand and a choice of holiday parks. Ilfracombe, originally a Victorian resort, with an annual Victorian festival, provides all kinds of family entertainment. An experience not to be missed is the cliff railway between the pretty little port of Lynmouth and its twin village of Lynton high on the cliff, with a backdrop of dramatic gorges or combes. In the centre of the county lies Dartmoor, with its wild open spaces, granite tors and spectacular moorland, rich in wildlife and ideal for walking, pony trekking and cycling.

Fairwater Head Hotel

3 Star Accommodation at Sensible Prices

75%

Located in the Devon/Dorset countryside, but close to Lyme Regis, this beautiful Edwardian Country House Hotel has all you need for a peaceful and relaxing break.

Dogs Most Welcome and Free of Charge
Countryside location with panoramic views • AA One Rosette Restaurant

Fairwater Head Hotel
Hawkchurch, Near Axminster, Devon EX13 5TX
Tel: 01297 678349 • Fax: 01297 678459
e-mail: stay@fairwaterheadhotel.co.uk
www.fairwaterheadhotel.co.uk

West Titchberry Farm

SB

Situated on the rugged North Devon coast, West Titchberry is a working traditionally run stock farm, half a mile from Hartland Point. The South West Coastal Path skirts around the farm making it an ideal base for walkers.

Pick ups and kit transfers available. Long term parking on site.

The three guest rooms comprise an en suite family room; one double and one twin room, with wash basins.

All rooms have colour TV, radio, hairdryer, tea/coffee making facilities; bathroom/toilet and separate shower room on the same floor plus a downstairs toilet.
Outside, guests may take advantage of a sheltered walled garden. Sorry, no pets.

Hartland village is 3 miles away, Clovelly 6 miles, Bideford and Westward Ho! 16 miles and Bude 18 miles.

- *B&B from £25–£30pppn • Evening meal £14*
- *Children welcome at reduced rates for under 11s*
- *Open all year except Christmas*

Mrs Yvonne Heard, West Titchberry Farm, Hartland Point, Near Bideford EX39 6AU

Tel & Fax: 01237 441287

The Mount, Northdown Road, Bideford EX39 3LP Tel: 01237 473748

A warm welcome awaits you at The Mount in the historic riverside town of Bideford. This small, interesting Georgian building is full of character and charm and is set in its own semi-walled garden, with a beautiful Copper Beech, making it a peaceful haven so close to the town. Within five minutes easy walking, you can be in the centre of the Old Town, with its narrow streets, quay, medieval bridge and park. The Mount is also an ideal centre for exploring the coast, countryside, towns and villages of North Devon. The quiet, restful bedrooms, (single, double, twin and family) are all en suite. Tea and coffee making facilities are available. All rooms have TV. Non-smoking. Bed and Breakfast £35 to £40 per person per night. Golfing breaks – discounted green fees

e-mail: andrew@themountbideford.co.uk
www.themountbideford.co.uk

Graham and Liz White, Bulworthy Cottage, Stony Cross, Alverdiscott, Near Bideford EX39 4PY
Tel: 01271 858441

SB

Once three 17th century miner's cottages, Bulworthy has been sympathetically renovated to modern standards whilst retaining many original features. Our twin and double guest rooms both offer en suite accommodation, with central heating, colour TV, and many other extras. Relax in the garden with views across the countryside to Exmoor. Standing in quiet countryside, Bulworthy is within easy reach of the moors, Tarka Trail, South West Coastal Path, Rosemoor and numerous National Trust properties. We offer a choice of breakfasts and evening meals, using home grown and local produce. A selection of wines and beers to complement your evening meal is available.

B&B from £32pppn.

e-mail: bulworthy@aol.com • www.bulworthycottage.co.uk

Little Bray House · North Devon

SB

Situated 9 miles east of Barnstaple, Little Bray House is ideally placed for day trips to North and East Devon, the lovely sandy surfing beaches at Saunton Sands and Woolacombe, and many places of interest both coastal and inland. Exmoor also has great charm. Come and share the pace of life and fresh air straight from the open Atlantic and be sustained by a good healthy breakfast. One twin-bedded flatlet with bathroom, or use the Self Catering accommodation in Orchard Cottage and Barn Cottage. Reasonable rates.

Brayford, near Barnstaple EX32 7QG
Tel: 01598 710295
e-mail: holidays@littlebray.co.uk
www.littlebray.co.uk

Brixham, Colyton

SB

SB

The Oyster is a modern bungalow in the pretty, peaceful village of Colebrooke in the heart of Mid Devon. There is a spacious garden for children to play around or sit on the patio. Comfortable accommodation with tea/coffee making facilities, with TV in bedroom and lounge. Bedrooms en suite or with private bathroom - two double and one twin. Walking distance to the New Inn, Coleford, a lovely 13th century free house. Dartmoor and Exmoor are only a short drive away. Central heating. Open all year. Ample parking. Terms from £25 per person for Bed and Breakfast. Children and pets welcome. Smoking accepted.

The Oyster
01363 84576

To find us take the Barnstaple road (A377)out of Crediton, turn left after one-and-a-half miles at sign for Colebrooke and Coleford. In Coleford village turn left at the crossroads, then in Colebrooke village take the left hand turning before the church, the Oyster is the second on the right.

Pearl Hockridge, The Oyster, Colebrooke, Crediton EX17 5JQ

Hayne Farm

Cheriton Fitzpaine
Crediton EX17 4HR

Occupied by members of the same family since the 17th century, Hayne Farm is sited in a quiet lane with its own extensive gardens, summer house, small wood and duck pond. It is the ideal setting for a relaxing break or holiday.

Many charming features include an oak beamed fireplace, and lounge with easy chairs and television. Three bedrooms, two with double beds and a third en suite family room. All have tea and coffee making facilities. Children are welcome and cot, high chair and baby sitting can be provided. No smoking or pets.

There are many places to see in the area including National Trust houses and gardens. Exmoor and Dartmoor are within easy driving time as are the north and south Devon coasts. The cathedral city of Exeter is a 30 minute drive away and provides shopping and entertainment.

Full cooked breakfasts are provided for guests, and local pubs are within easy reach for evening meals. Packed lunches are available on request; evening meals by prior arrangement.

Bed & Breakfast from £28.00, reductions for children.

Mrs M Reed • Tel: 01363 866392

symbols

 Totally non-smoking

 Children Welcome

 Suitable for Disabled Guests

 Pets Welcome

SB *Short Breaks available*

 Licensed

SB

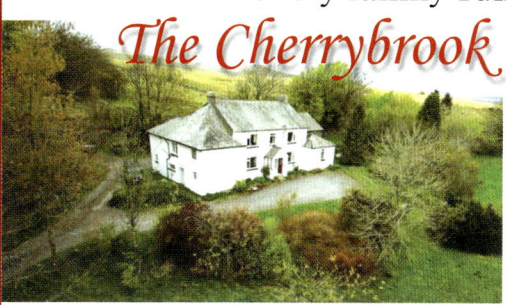

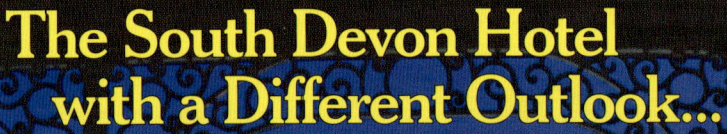

The Red Lion

has been offering generous hospitality since 1750 when it was a Coaching House. Log fires and gleaming brass in a friendly old bar, hearty English breakfasts, terraced gardens overlooking the River Dart, and an exceptionally warm welcome all await you.

Bedrooms are individually furnished, with comfortable beds, central heating, colour TV, tea-making facilities and telephones. An extensive menu includes daily specials and features fresh produce, prime local meats, fresh fish and locally grown vegetables. Picturesque countryside and a mild climate make this a perfect holiday retreat.

SB

Exmouth, Ilfracombe

Lynmouth/Lynton

SB

Blue Ball Inn
formerly The Exmoor Sandpiper Inn

is a romantic Coaching Inn dating in part back to the 13th century, with low ceilings, blackened beams, stone fireplaces and a timeless atmosphere of unspoilt old world charm. Offering visitors great food and drink, a warm welcome and a high standard of accommodation.

The inn is set in an imposing position on a hilltop on Exmoor in North Devon, a few hundred yards from the sea, and high above the twin villages of Lynmouth and Lynton, in an area of oustanding beauty.

The spectacular scenery and endless views attract visitors and hikers from all over the world.

We have 16 en suite bedrooms, comfortable sofas in the bar and lounge areas, and five fireplaces, including a 13th century inglenook. Our extensive menus include local produce wherever possible, such as locally reared meat, amd locally caught game and fish, like Lynmouth Bay lobster; specials are featured daily. We also have a great choice of good wines, available by the bottle or the glass, and a selection of locally brewed beers, some produced specially for us.

Stay with us to relax, or to follow one of the seven circular walks through stunning countryside that start from the Inn. Horse riding for experienced riders or complete novices can be

arranged. Plenty of parking. Dogs (no charge), children and walkers are very welcome!

Blue Ball Inn formerly The Exmoor Sandpiper Inn
Countisbury, Lynmouth, Devon EX35 6NE
01598 741263
www.BlueBallinn.com • www.exmoorsandpiper.com

Woody Bay, Parracombe
Devon EX31 4RA
01598 763224

Moorlands, formerly the Woody Bay Station Hotel, is a family-run Guesthouse in a most beautiful part of North Devon, surrounded by Exmoor countryside and within two miles of the spectacular coastline.

Very comfortable and quiet single, double or family suite accommodation, all en suite with bath or shower, colour TV with DVD and beverage making facilities.

Moorlands has a licensed dining room and residents' lounge with open fire, all set in six acres of gardens. A perfect retreat for the country lover to relax and unwind.

Bed and Breakfast £33 - £39.50pppn.
Evening meals by arrangement from £16.
Some ground floor rooms and
self-catering apartments available.
Please see our website for special offers.
www.moorlandshotel.co.uk

BRENDON HOUSE
Brendon, Lynton, Devon EX35 6PS
Tel: 01598 741206
e-mail: brendonhouse4u@aol.com
www.brendonhouse4u.com

Brendon House is a licensed country guesthouse with five well appointed en suite bedrooms with colour TV and tea/coffee making facilities. There is a residents' lounge with log fire in the winter months, and an award-winning restaurant serving local food and game and home grown seasonal vegetables from the garden.

Sitting in almost an acre of mature gardens, Brendon House provides the ideal location to just relax and unwind or as a base from which to explore the beautiful countryside, walks and views of the Exmoor National Park and the rugged North Devon coast

Lynmouth/Lynton

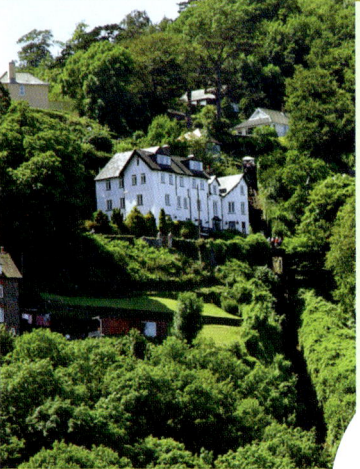

Lynmouth/Lynton

Hillside House

Situated on the East Lyn River at Lynmouth, in a perfect position to explore an abundance of coastal, riverside and woodland scenery. Hillside House is ideally suited to the needs of walkers or those of a less strenuous disposition. Double, twin or single rooms are available, each has a TV, hair-dryer, tea/coffee making facilities and either en suite or private bath/shower room. We offer a four-course breakfast in our dining-room where a large selection of books and magazines are available. Well behaved dogs are welcome. Packed lunches on request. Kit transfer can be arranged. Non-smoking.

**22 Watersmeet Road, Lynmouth, Devon EX35 6EP
Tel: 01598 753836
e-mail: info@hillside-lynmouth.co.uk
www.hillside-lynmouth.co.uk**

The Heatherville

The Heatherville invites you to our peaceful and relaxing home. Arrive to a warm welcome. This lovely Victorian villa has in recent years been restored to a very high standard giving a feeling of luxury and elegance without losing the charm of a large country house. Come and share our wonderful stunning views. We are in a quiet location, overlooking the River Lyn and surrounding woodland and yet only four minutes' walk from the heart of Lynmouth. With our own private parking adjacent, we are a cosy six bedroom hotel, here to provide you with a warm and friendly service. With your comfort in mind, our hotel is a non-smoking residence. Double rooms from £80.
We aim to retain a personal, caring touch to ensure your stay is a memorable one.

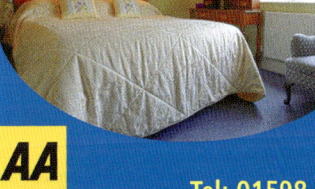

**Tel: 01598 752327 • Fax: 01598 753893
Tors Park, Lynmouth, Devon EX35 6NB
e-mail: theheatherville@aol.com • www.theheatherville.co.uk**

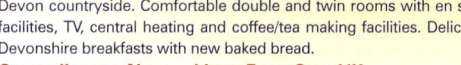

Okehampton, Ottery St Mary

PARSONAGE FARM

A warm welcome awaits you at our family-run organic farm, situated approximately one mile from the picturesque village of Iddesleigh where there is an excellent 15th century inn called the Duke of York. The ancient market town of Hatherleigh is three miles away and has a weekly market and auction. The Tarka Trail passes through our farmyard, and 400m of salmon trout fishing is available on the farm boundary, where there is a fishing hut, a secluded spot for a picnic (chairs and table provided.) There are other walks around the farm with an abundance of wildlife and flowers and a chance to watch the cows being milked from a gallery. RHS Rosemoor is about 8 miles away and the nearest surfing beaches are on the North Devon and North Cornwall coast. An ideal peaceful haven for touring both Devon and Cornwall, including Dartmoor and Exmoor.

Guests are able to relax in the lounge with large screen digital television and keyboard. Alternatively one can unwind in our large walled garden with a large swing hammock at the rear of the house overlooking the fish pond and magnificent view of Iddesleigh. Accommodation consists of a two-bedroom family room en suite and a double room en suite, both with tea/coffee making facilities, central heating, digital TV and WiFi. There is a games room with table tennis, darts, running machine, snooker or pool. B & B from £30pp for double room, £35 pp for single room. Open Easter – October. No smoking and no pets. Reduction for weekly bookings and children.

Mrs Rosemary Ward, Parsonage Farm, Iddesleigh, Winkleigh, Devon EX19 8SN
Tel: 01837 810318 • e-mail: roseward01@yahoo.co.uk
www.devon-holiday.com/parsonage

Peace and Tranquillity are easily found at

A delightful 16th century Devon longhouse in the beautiful Otter Valley

Fluxton Farm

SB

Occupying a sheltered position just south of Ottery St Mary, and only 4 miles from the sea at Sidmouth. We are no longer a working farm, but keep ducks and chickens and have lots of cats. We have 7 bedrooms, all en suite, and two charming sitting rooms. Our beamed dining room has a large open fireplace and separate tables, where a full English breakfast is served.

The house stands in peaceful, lawned gardens with a small trout stream flowing through.

As well as peace and quiet, we offer a warm welcome and an easy-going atmosphere.

• Children over 8 only.
• Pets welcome
(not in public rooms)

AA ★★

Fluxton Farm, Ottery St Mary
Devon EX11 1RJ
Tel: 01404 812818 • Fax: 01404 814843
Proprietor Ann Forth • www.fluxtonfarm.co.uk

Paignton

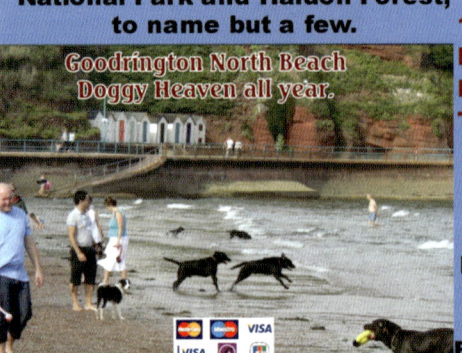

Plymouth

Seaton, Sidmouth

Beaumont, Castle Hill, Seaton EX12 2QW

Spacious and gracious Victorian, seafront guesthouse in a quiet East Devon town on England's only World Heritage coastline. Shopping, restaurants and leisure facilities nearby. Unrivalled views over Lyme Bay and Beer Cliffs.
Half-mile promenade just yards away.
All five rooms en suite with TV, Wi-Fi access,
tea and coffee making facilities, radio and hairdryer.
Parking available. Bed and Breakfast from £35 per person per night.
Special weekly rate. A warm welcome is assured.

Gill and Dave Fitzgerald • 01297 20832
e-mail: beaumont.seaton@talktalk.net
www.smoothhound.co.uk/hotels/beaumon1.html

The Groveside is a privately owned and run Guest House, entirely non-smoking, currently offering Bed and Breakfast throughout the year. We are a few minutes' level walk from the town centre and seafront.

Spacious, centrally heated en suite bedrooms have colour television, clock radio and tea and coffee making facilities. The guest lounge is comfortably furnished, with many personal touches. It is the perfect place to relax, read a book, watch the television, or plan your day out in Sidmouth or the surrounding area.

In the dining room enjoy a leisurely breakfast, with a wide choice from the buffet table followed by a full English breakfast.

We offer ample private car parking, but with Sidmouth shops, beaches and gardens all within easy walking distance from our

AA
★★★★
Guest House

Bed and Breakfast, who needs their car?
The Groveside is our home and as our guests we hope you will enjoy your stay with us.

Vicarage Road, Sidmouth EX10 8UQ
Tel: 01395 513406
www.thegroveside.co.uk

Sidmouth

SB

LOWER PINN FARM Peak Hill, Sidmouth EX10 0NN
Tel: 01395 513733
e-mail: liz@lowerpinnfarm.co.uk • www.lowerpinnfarm.co.uk

19th century built farmhouse on the World Heritage Jurassic Coast, two miles west of the unspoilt coastal resort of Sidmouth and one mile to the east of the pretty village of Otterton. Ideally situated for visiting many places, and for walking, with access to coastal path.

Comfortable, centrally heated en suite rooms with colour television and hot drink making facilities. Guests have their own keys and may return at all times throughout the day. Good hearty breakfast served in the dining room. Ample off-road parking.

Children and pets welcome.
Lower Pinn is a no smoking establishment.
Open all year.

B&B from £30 to £38

SB

Pinn Barton, Peak Hill, Sidmouth EX10 0NN

Peace, comfort and a warm welcome where we offer the little extras that attract guests back time and time again. Two miles from Sidmouth seafront. Lovely coastal walks and views from the farm. Warm and comfortable en suite bedrooms with TV, fridge, beverage trays and access at all times.

Open all year • No smoking
Children welcome

One twin, one double and
one family room available.
Terms from £32 to £36 per person.

Mrs Betty S. Sage
Tel & Fax: 01395 514004
e-mail: betty@pinnbartonfarm.co.uk
www.pinnbartonfarm.co.uk

Sidmouth, South Molton

The Longhouse • Salcombe Hill, Sidmouth

Formerly a part of the Norman Lockyer Observatory, The Longhouse has been lovingly restored and recently updated to provide the benefits of modern living. Surrounded by woodland, it is just under a mile from the town centre and sea front in easy reach of the town's facilities.

SB

- Ample private off-road parking available.
- All rooms have en suite showers.
- Tea/coffee making facilities, TV and DVD.
- Aga-cooked full English breakfast, using fresh local produce.
- Towels and linen supplied.

★★★★★
BED & BREAKFAST

A warm welcome is guaranteed, please phone and speak to Lynne or Pete Vincent for further booking information, tariff and availability.
Tel: 01395 577973 • www.holidaysinsidmouth.co.uk

Partridge Arms Farm

Yeo Mill, West Anstey, South Molton, North Devon EX36 3NU

Now a working farm of over 200 acres, four miles west of Dulverton, "Partridge Arms Farm" was once a coaching inn and has been in the same family since 1906. Genuine hospitality and traditional farmhouse fare awaits you. Comfortable accommodation in double, twin and single rooms, which have en suite facilities. There is also an original four-poster bedroom. Children welcome • Animals by arrangement • Residential licence • Open all year Fishing and riding available nearby • Group Bookings taken • FARM HOLIDAY GUIDE DIPLOMA WINNER.

Bed and Breakfast from £28; Evening Meal £16.   **Hazel Milton • 01398 341217**
Fax: 01398 341569 • e-mail: bangermilton@hotmail.com
TOURIST ASSOCIATION

A useful index of towns/counties appears on pages 393-396

FHG Guides publish a large range of well-known accommodation guides. We will be happy to send you details or you can use the order form at the back of this book.

Tiverton, Topsham

The Mill

A warm welcome awaits you at our converted mill, beautifully situated on the banks of the picturesque River Exe. Close to the National Trust's Knightshayes Court and on the route of the Exe Valley Way. Easy access to both the north and south coasts, Exmoor and Dartmoor. Only two miles from Tiverton.

- Relaxing and friendly atmosphere with delicious farmhouse fare.
- En suite bedrooms with TV and tea/coffee making facilities.
- *Bed and Breakfast from £26.*

Mrs L. Arnold, The Mill, Lower Washfield, Tiverton EX16 9PD
Tel: 01884 255297
e-mail: themillwashfield@hotmail.co.uk
www.themill-tiverton.co.uk

The Globe Hotel
Topsham, Exeter, Devon EX3 0HR
Tel: 01392 873471

Discover Topsham and Discover The Globe,
a Traditional Inn situated in the centre of Topsham,
Exeter's Historic and Beautiful Estuary Town.

The Globe has 19 en suite bedrooms, some with four-posters, two ground floor rooms and serviced apartments in a nearby annex.

The Café Restaurant offers a taste of the West Country whilst the Inn Bar serves local ales, wines and juices.

Topsham Ales Community Brewery is housed in The Globe courtyard. Bike hire is available at the Globe's Route 2 Café Bar giving the perfect chance to explore the Exe Estuary. Menus and tariffs are available on the website.

e-mail: sales@globehotel.com • www.globehotel.com

Torquay, Totnes, Yelverton

Heathcliff House 16 Newton Road, Torquay, Devon TQ2 5BZ
Telephone: 01803 211580 • Owners: Adrian & Terri Bailey

SB

This former vicarage is now a superbly appointed family-run B&B equipped for today yet retaining its Victorian charm. All the bedrooms have full en suite facilities, colour TV and drink making facilities. The elegant licensed bar boasts an extensive menu and unlike many establishments, the car park has sufficient space to accommodate all vehicles to eliminate roadside parking. Torquay's main beach, high street shops, entertainment and restaurants are all nearby and with full English breakfast included, it is easy to see why guests return time after time.

Tariff for B&B ranges between £25 and £37pppn.

e-mail: heathcliffhouse@btconnect.com
www.heathcliffhousehotel.co.uk

ORCHARD HOUSE
Horner, Halwell, Totnes, Devon TQ9 7LB
Telephone: 01548 821448
e-mail: orchard-house-halwell@hotmail.com
www.orchard-house-halwell.co.uk

Tucked away in a rural valley of the South Hams, only a short drive from sandy beaches and Dartmoor. With mature gardens and private parking surrounding the house, it is a peaceful location from which to enjoy your stay.

Luxury accommodation in three spacious and beautifully furnished rooms, all en suite with colour TV, clock radio, hair dryer and tea/coffee tray. Full central heating, sitting area has a log burner. Ample and varied breakfast using local produce. No smoking or pets.

From £27.50 to £30 pppn

Callisham Farm B&B
Rustic charm in rural Devon countryside

Esme Wills and her family extend a warm welcome to their guests all year round. Feel at home in one of the three comfortable en suite bedrooms, with tea/coffee tray, clock radio and TV. Relax in the warm and cosy guests' lounge.

A superb English breakfast is the perfect beginning to the day; vegetarian and special diets catered for on request.

With easy access to rolling moorland, Callisham is a perfect base for riding, fishing, golf, and touring the beautiful coasts of Devon and Cornwall. In the nearby village of Meavy, the Royal Oak offers a selection of real ales and fine food; other pubs within a mile and a half; Plymouth 12 miles.

www.callisham.co.uk • esme@callisham.co.uk
Meavy, Near Yelverton PL20 6PS • Tel/Fax: 01822 853901

Yelverton

Harrabeer Country House
Harrabeer Lane, Yelverton PL20 6EA

Quiet, family-run COUNTRY HOUSE offering versatile 4 star **in-house** and **self catering GUEST ACCOMMODATION** with many of the services of a small HOTEL. Restaurant (open to non-residents by arrangement). Licensed bar. Ideally situated for Dartmoor activities; only 9 miles from Plymouth.

01822 853302 • reception@harrabeer.co.uk • www.harrabeer.co.uk

Sampford Manor

Bed & Breakfast in the wilds of Dartmoor

Double or Twin Bedded rooms with private bathroom or shower.
£27.00-£40.00 per person per night.
Dogs welcome. Stabling or grazing for horses.

Sampford Manor, Sampford Spiney, Yelverton, Devon PL20 6LH • Tel: 01822 853442
e-mail: manor@sampford-spiney.fsnet.co.uk • www.sampford-spiney.fsnet.co.uk

The FHG Directory of Website Addresses
on pages 375-392 is a useful quick reference guide for holiday accommodation with e-mail and/or website details

Other British holiday guides from FHG Guides

PUBS & INNS · 300 GREAT HOTELS

SHORT BREAK HOLIDAYS

The bestselling and original PETS WELCOME!

THE GOLF GUIDE - Where to Play, Where to Stay

SELF-CATERING HOLIDAYS · 500 GREAT PLACES TO STAY

CARAVAN & CAMPING HOLIDAYS · FAMILY BREAKS

Published annually: available in all good bookshops or direct from the publisher:
FHG Guides, Abbey Mill Business Centre, Seedhill, Paisley PA1 1TJ
Tel: 0141 887 0428 • Fax: 0141 889 7204
e-mail: admin@fhguides.co.uk • www.holidayguides.com

Beaminster, Bournemouth

Dorset

Bournemouth

Bournemouth B&B
Southernhay Hotel
★★★ HOTEL

42 Alum Chine Rd, Westbourne,
Bournemouth BH4 8DX
Tel & Fax: 01202 761251

The Southernhay Hotel provides warm, friendly, high standard accommodation with a large car park and a hearty breakfast. All rooms have central heating, colour TV, tea/coffee making facilities and hairdryer. The hotel is ideally situated at the head of Alum Chine (a wooded ravine) leading down to the sea and miles of safe sandy beaches.

The Bournemouth International Centre, cinemas, theatres, restaurants, clubs and pubs are all within easy reach; minutes by car or the frequent bus service. Six bedrooms, four en suite. Open all year. Details from Tom and Lynn Derby. 2 for 1 Golf deals available

Bed and Breakfast from £20 to £30 per adult per night.

enquiries@southernhayhotel.co.uk • www.southernhayhotel.co.uk

---

Denewood is a smart, friendly family hotel, ideally situated to take advantage of the Bournemouth beaches and the new surf reef which are only 500 yards away, the popular Boscombe shopping centre and the famous Opera House. The hotel has a Health and Beauty salon offering a wide range of pampering treatments. For the business traveller there is a complete set of office facilities, plus internet access points.

**B&B from £22.50-£30.
Special weekly rates available
and Short Break discounts**

All 12 of our bedrooms, which are divided over 2 floors, are individually decorated and have a range of amenities such as a desk and chair, en suite facilities, tea and coffee making equipment and a television.

DENEWOOD HOTEL
40 Sea Road, Bournemouth BH5 1BQ
Tel: 01202 309913 • Fax: 01202 391155
www.denewood.co.uk

AA
Associate
Guest
Accommodation

★★★
GUEST
ACCOMMODATION

Bournemouth

Bournemouth, Bridport

Bridport

Dunster Farm

We invite you to relax and enjoy a carefree holiday in our 16th century farmhouse, situated in Broadoak, at the heart of the Marshwood Vale.

SB

Our home has lots of character with traditional oak beams and a log fire. Dunster Farm is a real working farm, and children who visit are most welcome to help collect eggs and watch the milking of cows. The heated bedrooms are all en suite, with radio clock alarm, TV and tea/coffee making. There is a lounge with TV. This is an ideal base for touring the South West, and the historic market town of Bridport is 4 miles away. The surrounding area offers activities such as horse riding , golf and fishing.

Dunster Farm, Broadoak, Bridport DT6 5NR
• Tel: 01308 424626 • Fax: 01308 423544
e-mail: dunsterfarm@onebillinternet.co.uk • www.dunsterfarm.co.uk

Britmead House
HOTEL
West Bay Road,
Bridport
Dorset DT6 4EG
Tel: 01308 422941
www.britmeadhouse.co.uk
e-mail: britmead@talk21.com

SB

An elegant Edwardian house, family-run and ideally situated between Bridport and West Bay Harbour, with its beaches, golf course, Chesil Beach and Dorset Coastal Path.
We offer full en suite rooms (two ground floor), all with TV, tea/coffee making facilities, and hairdryer. South-facing lounge and dining room overlooking the garden.
Private parking •Non-smoking • Free Wi-Fi

SB

Westwood House

29 High West Street, Dorchester DT1 1UP
01305 268018 • www.westwoodhouse.co.uk
reservations@westwoodhouse.co.uk

SB

Personally run by owners, Tom and Demelza Stevens, Westwood House offers comfortable, informal, non-smoking accommodation.
Each bedroom has digital TV, complimentary wi-fi, and tea/coffee making.
Breakfast is served in the light and airy conservatory.

A variety of pubs, restaurants and cafes are just a short stroll away.
The lovely market town of Dorchester has many places of historical interest, and is an ideal base for exploring the Dorset coast and countryside.

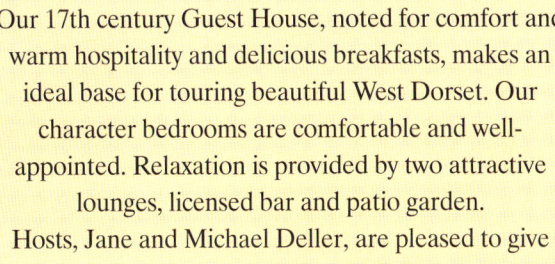

Dorchester

Portland, Sherborne, Shillingstone

Dorset has plenty to offer for an outdoor break. The spectacular cliffs of the Jurassic Coast, a World Heritage Site, form a major attraction for fossil hunters, particularly in the area around Charmouth and Lyme Regis. There are resorts to suit everyone, from traditional, busy Bournemouth with 10 kilometres of sandy beach and a wide choice of entertainment, shopping and dining, to the quieter seaside towns of Seatown, Mudeford and Barton-on-Sea, and Charmouth with its shingle beach. Lulworth Cove is one of several picturesque little harbours, and Weymouth, Lyme Regis and West Bay provide ideal facilities for sailing holidays. With almost half the county included in Areas of Outstanding Natural Beauty, walking enthusiasts have a choice of both coast and country, from cliff paths above the sea to rolling countryside, the Avon and Stour Valleys and fringes of the New Forest inland.

SB

Beech Farm

Sigwells, Charlton Horethorne, Near Sherborne
Dorset DT9 4LN • Mrs Susan Stretton

Comfortable farmhouse with relaxed atmosphere on our 140-acre farm, with beef and horses. A peaceful area on the Somerset/Dorset border with wonderful views from Corton Beacon.

*Four miles from the old abbey town of **Sherborne**, six miles from Wincanton, and just two miles off the A303.*

The farmhouse offers a double room en suite, a twin room, guest bathroom and an attic family room, all with TV and hospitality trays.

Bed and Breakfast £25 per person, less 10% for two or more nights.

Pets and horses by arrangement.
• Open all year except Christmas.

Tel: 01963 220524 • mobile: 07816 173657
e-mail: beechfarm@sigwells.co.uk
www.sigwells.co.uk

Our beautiful Listed farm house is ideally positioned in the glorious county of Dorset where many beauty spots are just waiting to be explored. Comfortable, well equipped and sleeping up to 5, we also serve a full English breakfast with various choices.
Guest sitting room • Large peaceful garden • Lovely walks

Contact Jill & Brian Miller, Lower Fifehead Farmhouse
Fifehead St Quinton, Sturminster Newton
Dorset DT10 2AP • Tel/Fax: 01258 817335
email: lowerfifeheadfarm@googlemail.com

SB

Sandhaven **Guest House**

You can be sure of a warm welcome with good home-cooking whenever you stay at Sandhaven. We wish to make sure your stay is as relaxing and enjoyable as possible. All bedrooms are en suite and equipped with tea and coffee making facilities; all have colour TV. There is a residents' lounge, dining room and conservatory for your comfort. The Purbeck Hills are visible from the guest house, as is the beach, which is only 100 metres away.

SB

- *Bed and Breakfast is available from £32.50 to £37.50.*
- *Non-smoking bedrooms.*
- *Open all year except Christmas.*

*Janet Foran • Sandhaven Guest House
5 Ulwell Road, Swanage BH19 1LE
Tel: 01929 422322*

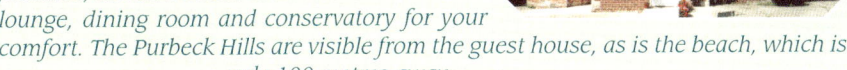

*e-mail: mail@sandhaven-guest-house.co.uk
www.sandhaven-guest-house.co.uk*

Wareham (near Lulworth)

Breachfield is a friendly and traditional B&B set in the heart of Wool, in the beautiful county of Dorset. It is ideally located as an excellent base to get to all the sights and attractions this area has to offer. The world famous Monkey World Ape Rescue Centre is just 2 minutes away.

www.breachfieldbedandbreakfast.co.uk

Our warm, cosy, country-syle rooms offer a superb base where you can unwind at the end of an action-packed day. We have a variety of rooms to suit all accommodation needs, ranging from single occupancy to family rooms, and we offer both en suite and private bathroom facilities.

Breachfield B&B, 9 Breachfield, Wool, Wareham BH20 6DQ

e-mail: matt@matthart9.wanadoo.co.uk • tel: 01929 405308 or 07776 043140

Luckford Wood Farmhouse
Church Street, East Stoke
Wareham, Dorset BH20 6AW

In the heart of Dorset countryside, very peaceful, recently refurbished, all en suite, free Wi-Fi. Extensive classical farmhouse breakfast served in dining room, conservatory (or garden). Ideal for cyclists, walkers, beach lovers, golfers. Tank Museum, Monkey World, Lulworth nearby. B&B from £30pppn, open all year. Caravan and camping available and storage.

Tel: 01929 463098 • Mobile: 07888 719002 / 07737 742615
e-mail: luckfordleisure@hotmail.co.uk • www.luckfordleisure.co.uk

symbols

 Totally non-smoking

 Children Welcome

 Suitable for Disabled Guests

 Pets Welcome

SB *Short Breaks available*

 Licensed

The ideal place to relax and unwind...

GRAYBANK

Lisa and Clive Orchard,
Graybank Bed and Breakfast,
Main Road, West Lulworth BH20 5RL
Tel: 01929 400256
e-mail: lisa@graybank.co.uk
www.graybank.co.uk

Children aged 12 and over welcome. We do not accept pets.
B&B from £40 per person per night.

Built in 1871, Graybank is set in the picturesque village of West Lulworth, a beautiful and quiet location just a short walk from the spectacular Lulworth Cove and the World Heritage Coastline.

Four double en suite guest rooms and one twin guest room. All rooms have flat screen TV with FreeSat, and tea/coffee making facilities.

Full breakfast menu with vegetarian options. Good choice of pubs, cafes and restaurants within walking distance.

Free parking for all guests. Strictly non-smoking throughout. Open all year, whatever the weather!

SB

Gloucestershire

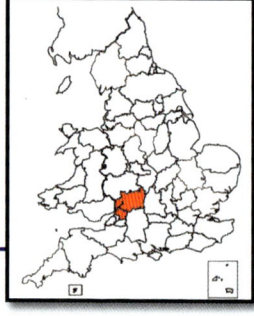

Cheltenham, Chipping Campden

Detmore House

Situated in an area of outstanding natural beauty, Detmore House is a period property set in extensive grounds. It offers spacious en suite rooms with TV, DVD, Wi-Fi and beautiful views. Close to Cheltenham and Gloucester, with restaurants, shops, racecourse and theatres, and a short walk from the Cotswold Way.

SB

London Road, Charlton Kings, Cheltenham GL52 6UT
01242 582868

gillkilminster@btconnect.com • www.detmorehouse.com

Individual, informal hotel owned and run by nice, friendly couple, keen to look after you. Close to Cheltenham's Regency splendour (town centre 2 miles), as well as idyllic Cotswold villages and countryside. Walkers welcome (Cotswold Way ¾ mile). Food sourced and cooked with care.

SB

Charlton Kings Hotel
London Road Cheltenham GL52 6UU
Tel: 01242 231061
enquiries@charltonkingshotel.co.uk
www.charltonkingshotel.co.uk

Parkview is a fine Regency guesthouse which stands in Cheltenham's nicest area, only 10 minutes' walk from the centre. The bedrooms are large and airy and have TV, tea, coffee and provide views onto Pittville Park. Cheltenham is famous for horse racing and festivals of music and literature, and two theatres provide a regular programme of entertainment.
Nearby Prestbury is the most haunted village in England, the Cotswold villages stand in the surrounding hills, and Stratford is one hour's drive.

Parkview Guesthouse

4 Pittville Crescent, Cheltenham GL52 2QZ • Tel: 01242 575567
e-mail: stay@parkviewguesthouse.me.uk • www.parkviewguesthouse.me.uk

Holly House

AA ★★★★ Bed & Breakfast

Ideally situated for touring the Cotswolds and Shakespeare's country. Double, twin and family rooms available, all beautifully appointed with en suite facilities. TV and tea and coffee. Private parking. Lovely garden room at guests' disposal. Village pub serves meals. Bike hire available locally.

Double room £65-£75 • Single room £55-£60 • Family room £80-£95 • Child reductions
Ebrington, Chipping Campden GL55 6NL   01386 593213
e-mail: info.hollyhouse@btinternet.com • www.hollyhousebandb.co.uk

Chipping Campden

Tel : 01452 840224

Quality all ground floor accommodation. "Kilmorie" is Grade II Listed (c1848) within conservation area in a lovely part of Gloucestershire. Double, twin, family or single bedrooms, all having tea tray, colour digital TV, radio, mostly en suite. Very comfortable guests' lounge, traditional home cooking is served in the separate diningroom overlooking large garden. Perhaps walk waymarked farmland footpaths which start here. Children may "help" with our pony, and "free range" hens. Rural yet perfectly situated to visit Cotswolds, Royal Forest of Dean, Wye Valley and Malvern Hills. Children over five years welcome. Hartpury College 3 miles. Ample parking.

Bed and full English Breakfast from £26 per person

SB

S.J. Barnfield, "Kilmorie Smallholding", Gloucester Road, Corse, Staunton, Gloucester GL19 3RQ
mobile: 07840 702218 • e-mail: sheila-barnfield@supanet.com

THE FOUNTAIN INN & LODGE

Parkend, Royal Forest of Dean, Gloucestershire GL15 4JD.

Traditional village inn, well known locally for its excellent meals and real ales. A Forest Fayre menu offers such delicious main courses as Lamb Shank with Redcurrant and Rosemary Sauce and Gloucester Sausage in Onion Gravy, together with a large selection of curries, vegetarian dishes, and other daily specials.

Centrally situated in one of England's foremost wooded areas, the inn makes an ideal base for sightseeing, or for exploring some of the many peaceful forest walks nearby.

All bedrooms (including one specially adapted for the less able) are en suite, decorated and furnished to an excellent standard, and have television and tea/coffee making facilities.

SB

Tel: 01594 562189 • Fax: 01594 564438 • e-mail: thefountaininn@aol.com • www.thefountaininnandlodge.com

---

Rose and Crown Inn

Playley Green, Redmarley D'Abitot,
Gloucestershire GL19 3NB
Tel. 01531 650234

enquiries@roseandcrownredmarley.co.uk • www.roseandcrownredmarley.co.uk

A traditional friendly country pub and dining room, easily accessible from Gloucester, Cheltenham, Ross-on-Wye and Tewkesbury. Choose to dine in the charming, rustic bar area or the beautiful dining room. Home-cooked food, prepared with fresh local ingredients. All British pub favourites are available, along with our ever-changing specials board. *B&B accommodation available.*

FHG Guides publish a large range of well-known accommodation guides. We will be happy to send you details or you can use the order form at the back of this book.

The FHG Directory of Website Addresses

on pages 375-392 is a useful quick reference guide for holiday accommodation with e-mail and/or website details

The *Laurels* at Inchbrook

A comfortable, rambling house, cottage and garden set beside the Inch Brook and adjoining fields. Lovely secluded garden, with badgers and bats: the stream is an otter route, and many birds come to visit us. Pets are most welcome, and there are dozens of splendid walks and the National Trust's Woodchester Park on our doorstep.

Nailsworth, a fashionable Cotswold town and a centre for excellence when it comes to eating out, is just under a mile away.

Ideally placed for exploring the West Country, Bath and Forest of Dean as well as the Cotswolds, our house is perfect for groups and family gatherings. Brochure on request. Self-catering facilities may be available at certain times of the year.

4 double (one ground floor accessible), 2 twin, 2 family;
all en suite, with TV, radio/alarm, tea/coffee facilities.
Full English, Vegetarian or Continental breakast.
Secure parking. Pet-friendly.
No smoking. Children welcome. Open all year.

Cow Lane, Inchbrook, Nailsworth GL5 5HA
Tel: 01453 834021 • *laurelsinchbrook@tiscali.co.uk*
www.laurelsinchbrook.co.uk

THE Old Stocks
Hotel, Restaurant & Bar
The Square,
Stow-on-the-Wold GL54 1AF

Ideal base for touring this beautiful area.
Tasteful guest rooms in keeping with
the hotel's old world character, yet with
modern amenities. 3-terraced patio garden with smoking area.

Mouth-watering menus offering a wide range of choices.

Special bargain breaks also available.

Tel: 01451 830666
Fax: 01451 870014
e-mail: fhg@oldstockshotel.co.uk
www.oldstockshotel.co.uk

Aston House, Broadwell, Moreton-In-Marsh GL56 0TJ

ASTON HOUSE is in the peaceful village of
Broadwell, one-and-a-half miles from Stow-
on-the-Wold, four miles from Moreton-in-
Marsh. It is centrally situated for all the Cotswold
villages, while Blenheim Palace, Warwick Castle,
Oxford, Stratford-upon-Avon, Cheltenham and
Gloucester are within easy reach.

Accommodation comprises a twin-bedded and a double room, both en suite on the first floor, and
a double room with private bathroom on the ground floor. All
rooms have tea/coffee making facilities, radio, colour TV,
hairdryer, electric blankets for the colder nights and fans for hot
weather. Bedtime drinks and biscuits are provided. Open from
March to October. No smoking. Car essential, parking. Pub
within walking distance. Wi-Fi, PC and internet access available.

*Bed and good English breakfast from £70 to £80 per room
per night; weekly from £475 to £520 per room.*

Tel: 01451 830475
e-mail: fja@astonhouse.net • www.astonhouse.net
VisitBritain ★★★★ Silver Award • AA ★★★★

Stow-on-the-Wold, Stroud

Bed and Full English Breakfast from £25 (reductions for children)

A traditional farmhouse with spectacular views of Cotswold countryside. Quiet location one mile from Stow. Ideally situated for exploring all Cotswold villages including Bourton-on-the-Water, Broadway, Burford and Chipping Campden. Within easy reach of Cheltenham, Oxford and Stratford-upon-Avon; also places of interest such as Blenheim Palace, Warwick Castle and many National Trust houses and gardens. Family, twin and double bedrooms; mostly en suite. TV, tea tray and hairdryer in all rooms. Relaxing guest lounge/dining room with Free Wi-Fi. Excellent pub food five minutes' walk away. Children welcome. Open all year.

★★★ Farmhouse

AA ★★★ Farmhouse

SB

Robert Smith and Julie-Anne, Corsham Field Farmhouse, Bledington Road, Stow-on-the-Wold GL54 1JH • 01451 831750 • Fax: 01451 832247
e-mail: farmhouse@corshamfield.co.uk • www.corshamfield.co.uk

The Withyholt Guest House

Paul Mead, Edge Near Stroud, Gloucestershire, GL6 6PG

★★★★ BED & BREAKFAST

AA ★★★★ Guest House

SB

Welcome to Withyholt Guest House

We offer bed and breakfast accommodation in a large house located near Stroud in Gloucestershire close to Gloucester Cathedral, Tetbury. Near Stroud in the heart of the Cotswold Hills. Many lovely country walks.

• En suite bedrooms • Private sitting room • Large garden • Snooker room • Drying room • Packed lunch if requested the night before.

Telephone: 01452 813618
Fax: 01452 812375
e-mail: info@thewithybedandbreakfast.com
www.thewithyholtbedandbreakfast.com

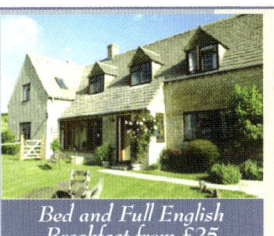

Just to the north of Bath, Gloucestershire forms the major part of the Cotswolds Area of Outstanding Natural Beauty, with gently rolling hills, sleepy villages and market towns full of character, ideal for a relaxing break whatever the season. There are gardens to visit, country pubs, antique shops, cathedrals and castles, as well as all kinds of outdoor activities, from 4x4 off-road driving to all the watersports on offer at the Cotswold Water Park, in the south east corner of the county. The Forest of Dean is another area well worth visiting for the wide variety of spring flowers and amazing autumn colours in the ancient woodlands.

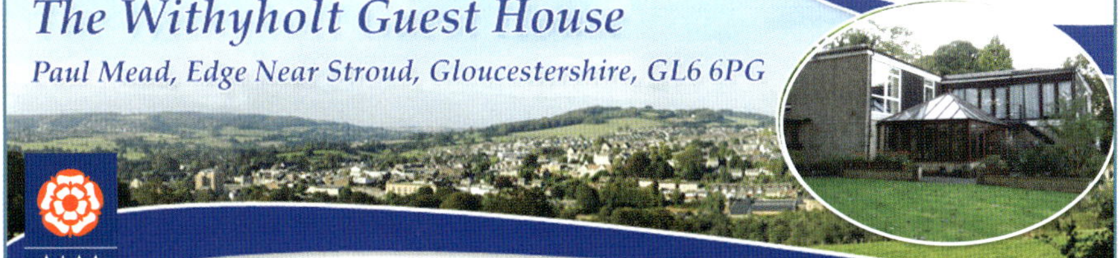

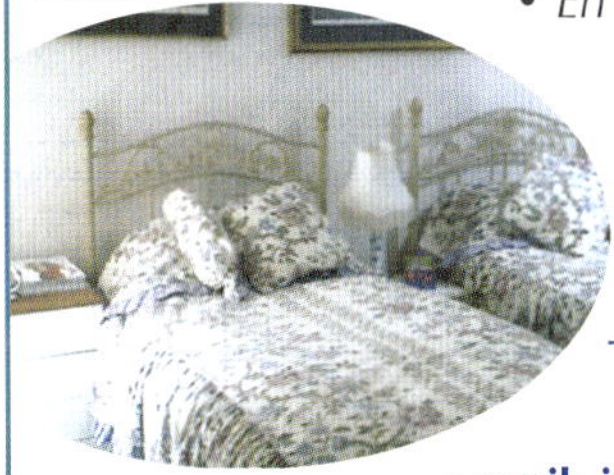

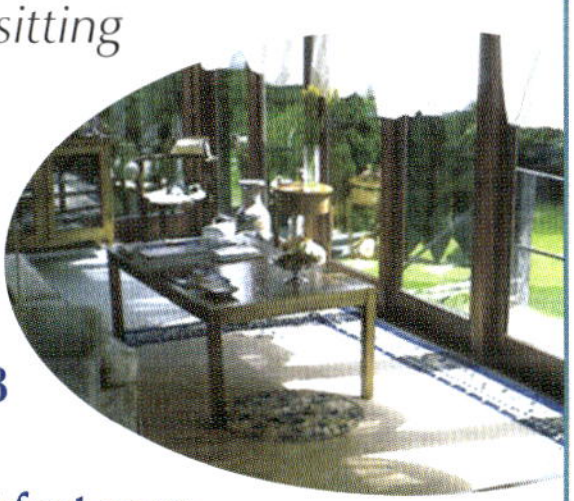

Upper Hasfield, Winchcombe

SB

Situated in pretty rural hamlet in gorgeous location close to Gloucester, Ledbury and Tewkesbury. Ideal walking country, Severn Way, and Malvern Hills. Double or twin en suite room in annex nearby, twin or double available in house. Horse riding and other leisure pursuits within easy reach. Excellent local pubs. Dogs welcome by arrangement
A warm welcome awaits you..

**Mike and Liz Dawson, Rusts Meadow Hasfield Road, Upper Hasfield, Gloucestershire GL19 4LL
Tel: 01452 700814**

Ireley is an 18th century farmhouse located in the heart of gentle countryside, one-and-a-half miles from Winchcombe and within easy reach of Cheltenham, Gloucester, Stratford-upon-Avon and Worcester.

The cosy yet spacious guest rooms (one double and two twin) offer either en suite or private bathroom. Relax in the evening beside a traditional open fire and in the morning enjoy a delicious English breakfast. Families are welcome, to enjoy the unique atmosphere of this working farm.

**Mrs Margaret Warmington, Ireley Farm, Broadway Road, Winchcombe GL54 5PA
Tel: 01242 602445 • e-mail: warmingtonmaggot@aol.com**

B&B from £28.50 per person.

Bath

Somerset

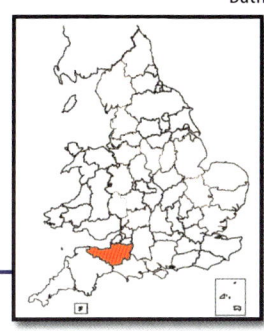

Eden Vale Farm

Eden Vale Farm nestles down in a valley by the River Frome. Enjoying a picturesque location, this old watermill offers a selection of rooms including en suite facilities, complemented by an excellent choice of full English or Continental breakfasts. Beckington is an ideal centre for visiting Bath, Longleat, Salisbury, Cheddar, Stourhead and many National Trust Houses including Lacock Village.

Only a ten minute walk to the village pub, three-quarters of a mile of river fishing. Local golf courses and lovely walks.

Very friendly animals. Dogs welcome.

Open all year.

Mrs Barbara Keevil, Eden Vale Farm, Mill Lane, Beckington, Near Frome BA11 6SN • Tel: 01373 830371
e-mail: bandb@edenvalefarm.co.uk • www.edenvalefarm.co.uk

SB

The Old Red House

Welcome to our romantic Victorian "Gingerbread" house which is colourful, comfortable and warm; full of unexpected touches and intriguing little curiosities. The leaded and stained glass windows are now double glazed to ensure a peaceful night's stay. Each bedroom is individually furnished, some with antiques and a king-size bed. All have colour TV with Freeview, complimentary beverages, radio alarm clock, hairdryer and either en suite shower or private bathroom. Easy access to city centre, via road or river paths. The English breakfast and buffet will keep you going all day. We have private parking. Non-smoking.

Theresa Elly, The Old Red House, 37 Newbridge Road,
Bath BA1 3HE • 01225 330464
e-mail: theoldredhousebath@onebillinternet.co.uk
www.theoldredhousebath.co.uk

Bath

Marlborough House
1 Marlborough Lane, Bath BA1 2NQ
Tel: +44 (0)1225 318175 • Fax: +44 (0)1225 466127

Marlborough House is an enchanting, Victorian Guest House located at the edge of Royal Victoria Park, close to the heart of Georgian Bath and all the major attractions.

Each bedroom is handsomely furnished with antiques and contains either an antique wood four-poster, or a Victorian brass and iron bed. All are comfortable and scrupulously clean, with complimentary sherry and a hostess tray. Each has direct-dial telephone, wifi, alarm/radio, hairdryer, and colour TV.

Served in either the elegant parlour or lovely dining room, breakfasts are cooked to order, using only the highest quality organic ingredients.

www.marlborough-house.net

Steve and Anna Wynne welcome you to their guest house. Very conveniently located five minutes' walk to the city and all of Bath's famous attractions. Close to the Kennet and Avon canal (Bath in Bloom winners.) All rooms en suite, with central heating, TV, tea/coffee facilities. Traditional cooked breakfast or Continental breakfasts. Ground floor rooms.

B&B single from £35, double/twin from £27pp. Min. 2 nights stay.

The White Guest House

Free bottle of wine when you mention 'FHG'

23 Pulteney Gardens, Bath BA2 4HG
01225 426075
enquiries@whiteguesthouse.co.uk
www.whiteguesthouse.co.uk

Bath

SB

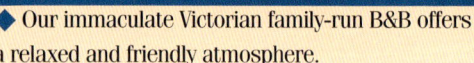

Dulverton

SB

Find our 17th century farmhouse hidden amid picturesque countryside two miles south-west of Dulverton - off the beaten track.

Welcome to Higher Langridge Farm, offering Farmhouse Bed & Breakfast near Dulverton, the southern gateway to Exmoor.

On a family-run working farm on the Devon/ Somerset border, our 17th century farmhouse is secluded in peaceful, quiet countryside and enjoys spectacular views.

Prices from £35 based on two sharing

Just two miles off the A396 at Exebridge, very accessible, and a short drive from Dulverton, a small, friendly Exmoor town with an interesting selection of gift shops, tea rooms, pubs and restaurants. The surrounding landscape is home to many wild animals, including red deer, often seen from the farmhouse.

Mike & Gill Summers, Higher Langridge Farm, Exebridge, Dulverton TA22 9RR • 01398 323999
e-mail: info@langridgefarm.co.uk
www.langridgefarm.co.uk

Higher Langridge Farm

Winsbere House

SB

Attractive private house set in pretty gardens on the edge of Dulverton, 10 minute walk from the centre and a short drive to Tarr Steps and the moors. Comfortable, tastefully decorated rooms with lovely country views and a friendly informal atmosphere. One double, one twin, both en suite, plus one double/single with private bathroom. Superb full English breakfast.

Cyclists welcome. Route Three West Country Way on doorstep. Ample private parking and lock-up cycle shed.

No dogs • Non-smoking • Children welcome aged 8 or over. • Excellent location for touring Exmoor, West Somerset and North Devon.

Open all year (except Christmas and New Year). Terms: £25 to £30pppn (single from £30).

Mrs M. Rawle, Winsbere House, Dulverton, Exmoor, Somerset TA22 9HU (01398 323278)
e-mail: info@winsbere.co.uk
www.winsbere.co.uk

SB

Yarn Market Hotel
25-31 High Street
Dunster
TA24 6SF
Tel: 01643 821425

The Yarn Market Hotel is a comfortable, family-run hotel which provides a friendly, relaxed atmosphere. Situated at the centre of a quaint English village it is an ideal location for walking and exploring Exmoor, the surrounding coastline and the many local attractions. All rooms are en suite, with tea and coffee making facilities and colour TV. Some have four-poster beds while others have spectacular views over the surrounding countryside. Family rooms are also available. The restaurant offers a mouth watering selection of dishes featuring local produce whenever possible. Packed lunches and drying facilities are also available.

Non-smoking. Well behaved pets are welcome.
Party bookings and midweek breaks a speciality.
B&B from £40.

e-mail: hotel@yarnmarkethotel.co.uk
www.yarnmarkethotel.co.uk

SB

North Down Farm

In tranquil, secluded surroundings on the Somerset/ Devon Border. Traditional working farm set in 150 acres of natural beauty with panoramic views of over 40 miles, on the edge of Exmoor. M5 7 miles, Taunton 10 miles. All rooms tastefully furnished to high standard include en suite, TV, and tea/coffee facilities. Double, twin or single rooms available. Dining room and lounge with log fires for our guests' comfort; centrally heated and double glazed. Drying facilities. Delicious home produced food a speciality. Fishing, golf, horse riding and country sports nearby. Dogs welcome.

Bed and Breakfast from £36 pppn,
Seven nights B&B and Evening Meals £295pp.
North Down Break: three nights B&B and Evening Meals £145 per person.

Jenny Cope, North Down Farm, Pyncombe Lane, Wiveliscombe,
Taunton TA4 2BL • Tel: 01984 623730
e-mail: jennycope@btinternet.com
www.north-down-farm.co.uk

Meare Manor

200-year-old Manor House set in own grounds with beautiful gardens and views over Mendip Hills. Peaceful setting in the heart of King Arthur country. Ideal base for tourist attractions including Glastonbury Abbey, Chalice Well, Wells Cathedral, Cheddar Gorge and Clarks Shopping Village. Warm welcome assured with friendly help and advice. Family rooms available. Hospitality trays, colour TV. Ample car parking. Open all year.

From M5, Junction 23 follow A39 Glastonbury - Street, take B3151 Glastonbury to Wedmore, approximately three miles from Glastonbury.
Bed and Breakfast from £70 double occupancy per night.

Sue Chapman, Meare Manor, 60 St Mary's Road, Meare, Glastonbury BA6 9SR • Tel 01458 860449 • Fax: 01458 860855
e-mail: reception@mearemanor.com • www.mearemanor.com

The Wayside Bed & Breakfast

Situated between Exmoor and the Coast, the ideal place for touring, walking, cycling or relaxing.
The accommodation is in an annexe to the main house giving you the freedom to come and go as you please.
Two light and airy double rooms, one with en suite shower room, the other with private bathroom.
Free Wi-Fi. Parking.

SB

Bilbrook, Minehead, Somerset TA24 6HE
Tel: 01984 641 669
e-mail: thewayside@tiscali.co.uk • www.thewayside.co.uk

Oakfield House

Northfield Road, Minehead TA24 5QH
Tel: 01643 704911 • www.oakfieldminehead.co.uk

SB

Oakfield House provides bed and breakfast accommodation in two double suites, comprising lounge and bedroom area both with en suite facilities, and views over the sea and surrounding countryside.
Situated on the lower slopes of the quiet North Hill, the house is only 200 metres from the sea front and just a short distance to all the local shops and amenities.
Prices from £32.50 per person per night. We are open all year.

The Old Mill

Bishop's Hull, Taunton TA1 5AB
Tel: 01823 289732 / 07967 673916
www.theoldmillbandb.co.uk
www.bandbtaunton.co.uk

Grade II Listed former Corn Mill, situated on the edge of a conservation village just two miles from Taunton. We have two lovely double bedrooms, The Mill Room with en suite facilities overlooking the weir pool, and The Cottage Suite with its own private bathroom, again with views over the river. Both rooms are centrally heated, with TV, generous beverage tray and thoughtful extras. Guests have their own lounge and dining area overlooking the river, where breakfast may be taken from our extensive breakfast menu amidst machinery of a bygone era. We are a non-smoking establishment.

Double from £27.50 – £32.50pppn
Single occupancy from £40 - £45

SB

Theale, Wells

Wells, Weston-Super-Mare, Williton

Wiltshire

SB

For the greatest concentration of prehistoric sites in Europe, visit Wiltshire. Most famous is the World Heritage Site, Stonehenge, on Salisbury Plain, dating back at least five thousand years, and with evidence of even earlier work.

Salisbury is the most well known centre in south Wiltshire, with its famous medieval cathedral, as well as individual shops in a historic setting. There is also the safari park at Longleat, farm parks, and stately homes and beautiful gardens to visit in the countryside, where there are also plenty of opportunities for walking and cycling.

Malmesbury, Marlborough

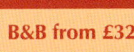

Scotland Lodge Farm

Warm welcome at family-run competition yard set in 46 acres of grassland. Lovely views and walks. Stonehenge and Salisbury nearby. Three attractive, comfortable rooms - double with private bathroom; twin and double on ground floor. Conservatory and garden for guests' use. Dogs by arrangement. French, Italian and German spoken. Easy access off A303 with entry through automatic gate. Excellent local pubs.

**Scotland Lodge Farm,
Winterbourne Stoke
Salisbury SP3 4TF
Tel: 01980 621199**

Mobile: 07763 083585 • e-mail: catherine.lockwood@bigwig.net

www.scotlandlodgefarm.co.uk

Spinney Farmhouse ~ Thoulstone, Chapmanslade, Westbury BA13 4AQ

Off A36, three miles west of Warminster; 16 miles from historic city of Bath. Close to Longleat, Cheddar and Stourhead. Reasonable driving distance to Bristol, Stonehenge, Glastonbury and the cathedral cities of Wells and Salisbury. Discounts on Longleat tickets.

• Washbasins, tea/coffee-making facilities and shaver points in all rooms.
• Family room available. • Guests' lounge with colour TV.
• Central heating. • Children and pets welcome.
• Ample parking. • Open all year. • No smoking

*Enjoy farm fresh food in a warm, friendly family atmosphere.
Bed and Breakfast from £26 per night. Reduction after 2 nights.
Evening Meal £12.*
Telephone: 01373 832412 • e-mail: isabelandbob@btinternet.com

---

HolidayGuides.com

Looking for holiday accommodation?

for details of hundreds of properties throughout the UK visit:

www.holidayguides.com

London
(Central & Greater)

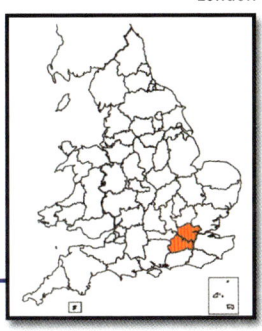

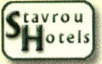

 # The Athena

110-114 SUSSEX GARDENS, HYDE PARK, LONDON W2 1UA
Tel: 0207 706 3866; Fax: 0207 262 6143
E-Mail: athena@stavrouhotels.co.uk www.stavrouhotels.co.uk

TREAT YOURSELVES TO A QUALITY HOTEL AT AFFORDABLE PRICES

The Athena is a newly completed family run hotel in a restored Victorian building. Professionally designed, including a lift to all floors and exquisitely decorated, we offer our clientele the ambience and warm hospitality necessary for a relaxing and enjoyable stay. Ideally located in a beautiful tree-lined avenue, extremely well-positioned for sightseeing London's famous sights and shops; Hyde Park, Madame Tussaud's, Oxford Street, Marble Arch, Knightsbridge, Buckingham Palace and many more are all within walking distance.

Travel connections to all over London are excellent, with Paddington and Lancaster Gate Stations, Heathrow Express, A2 Airbus and buses minutes away.
Our tastefully decorated bedrooms have en suite bath/shower rooms, satellite colour TV, bedside telephones, tea/coffee making facilities. Hairdryers, trouser press, laundry and ironing facilities available on request. Car parking available.

Stavrou Hotels is a family-run group of hotels.
We offer quality and convenience at affordable rates.
A VERY WARM WELCOME AWAITS YOU.

Single Rooms from £50-£89
Double/Twin Rooms from £64-£99
Triple & Family Rooms from £25 per person
All prices include full English breakfast plus VAT.

Our hotels accept all major Credit cards, but some charges may apply.

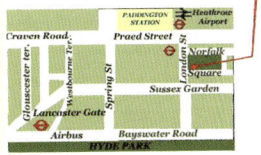

London

Berkshire

Eton

Whatever your interests, whether in the countryside or the town, Berkshire has much to offer. In the east of the county, just a short train ride away from central London, is Windsor Castle, the largest inhabited castle in the world. Racegoers will find plenty of action in Berkshire, with both Ascot and Royal Windsor in the east, and Newbury to the west, where you can also take a tour of the stables at Lambourn and watch the early morning gallops.

Terms quoted in this publication may be subject to increase if rises in costs necessitate

BLUEBELL HOUSE

LOVEL LANE, WOODSIDE, WINDSOR SL4 2DG
Tel & Fax: 01344 886828

Charming ex-coaching inn on the outskirts of Windsor and Ascot, and close to Bracknell and Maidenhead. Traditional rooms offering classic accommodation with an added touch of class.

All rooms tastefully furnished and have TV, hairdryer, trouserpress, iron, fridge, kettle and toaster. Close to Windsor, Legoland, racing and polo.

A very full Continental breakfast is taken in your room. Private off-road parking.

e-mail: registrations@bluebellhousehotel.co.uk
www.bluebellhousehotel.co.uk

SB

- Town centre location.
- Licensed bar and steam room.
- High quality accommodation at guest house prices.
- All rooms have en suite bathrooms, TV, tea/coffee making facilities, radio alarms, hairdryers, free wi-fi and internet.
- Heathrow Airport 25 minutes by car.
- Convenient for Legoland and trains to London.

Clarence Hotel
9 Clarence Road, Windsor, Berkshire SL4 5AE
Tel: 01753 864436 • Fax: 01753 857060 • www.clarence-hotel.co.uk

AA

---

symbols

 Totally non-smoking

 Children Welcome

 Suitable for Disabled Guests

 Pets Welcome

 SB *Short Breaks available*

 Licensed

Buckinghamshire

Only half an hour from London, the rolling hills and wooded valleys of the Buckinghamshire countryside provide a wonderful contrast to city life. Enjoy the bluebells in spring and the autumn colours of the woodland while following the innumerable footpaths, bridleways and National Trails that cross the county, looking at the local flora and fauna on the way.

There are fascinating historic towns and villages, including West Wycombe, owned by the National Trust, which also has many other interesting properties in the area. These include the stunning gardens at Cliveden, former home of the Astors and focus of the early twentieth century social scene. Shoppers will want to visit the complex at High Wycombe or for more specialised outlets, Amersham, the Georgian market town of Marlow, or Stony Stratford.

Barton-on-Sea, Hayling Island

Hampshire

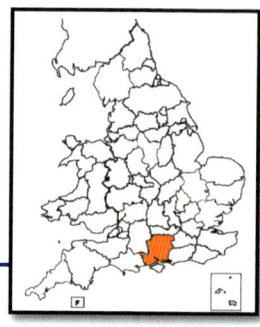

Ideally situated for the delights of the New Forest, scenic cliff top walks, local beaches, pleasure cruises to the Isle of Wight, the Needles and historic Hurst Castle, horse riding, cycling, golf and a whole host of indoor and outdoor pursuits. Laurel Lodge is a comfortable, centrally heated, converted bungalow, offering twin, double & family rooms. All rooms are fully en suite with tea and coffee making facilities, comfortable chairs, colour TV and alarm clock radio. Ground floor rooms available. Breakfast is served in our conservatory/diningroom with views over the garden.

Bed and Breakfast from £27.50 per person • Special deals for longer breaks • Children welcome, cot and high chair supplied by prior arrangement • Off-road parking for all rooms • Strictly no smoking • Open all year • Please phone for further details.

Laurel Lodge

Lee & Melanie Snook, Laurel Lodge,
48 Western Avenue, Barton-on-Sea, New Milton BH25 7PZ • 01425 618309

RAVENSDALE

- **double room from £66**
- **single room from £40**
- **triple room from £90**

Jane and Phil welcome you to their home, which is comfortably fitted and in a quiet location within a short walk of the beach and golf course. Two double rooms with en suite facilities; triple room with three single beds, use of main bathroom. Central heating, television, tea/coffee making facilities. A full English Breakfast is included and Evening Meal is optional. Car parking. No smoking, and no pets please. Children over 8 years,

Jane & Phil Taylor, Ravensdale,
19 St Catherines Road, Hayling Island PO11 0HF
Tel & Fax: 023 9246 3203 • Mobile: 07802 188259
www.ravensdale-hayling.co.uk

OAKLEA GUEST HOUSE

**London Road,
Hook RG27 9LA
Tel: 01256 762673
Fax: 01256 762150**
Please quote FHG

Friendly, family-run Guest House. All bedrooms en suite with TV and hospitality tray. Guest lounge with SKY TV, licensed bar. Easy access from J5 M3, London 55 minutes by train. Free wireless internet access available via own equipment.

GOLF: Many excellent courses within 10-mile radius.
HORSE RACING at Sandown, Ascot and Goodwood.
SHOPPING at The Oracle, Reading and Festival Place, Basingstoke.
DAYS OUT: Thorpe Park, Chessington, Legoland, Windsor Castle, Hampton Court, RHS Wisley, Milestones.

AA
★★★★
Guest House

e-mail: reception@oakleaguesthouse.co.uk • www.oakleaguesthouse.co.uk

Set in its own grounds in a quiet location, this delightful 1912 period house offers a friendly and relaxed atmosphere, a high standard of accommodation and ample parking.

A delicious choice of breakfasts is served in the spacious residents' dining room.

Only five minutes' walk from the High Street and Quay area, ideal for mariners and for travellers catching Isle of Wight ferries.

Delightful forest and coastal walks.
Open all year.

The Rowans, 76 Southampton Road, Lymington SO41 3GZ
Tel: 01590 672276 • Fax: 01590 688610 • e-mail: therowans@totalise.co.uk

AA
★★★★
Council
Accommodation

Harts Lodge

Bungalow (non-smoking), set in three acres. Large garden with small lake. Quiet location. Three miles west of Lymington. Friendly welcome. Double, twin and family en suite rooms, each with tea/coffee making facilities and colour TV. Delicious four-course English breakfast. The sea and forest are five minutes away by car. Horse riding, golf and fishing are nearby. The village pub, ½ mile serves excellent meals. Sorry, no pets. Bed and Breakfast from £30 per person.

**242 Everton Road, Everton,
Lymington, Hampshire SO41 0HE**

Tel: 01590 645902

SB

Lymington, Milford-on-Sea, New Forest

New Forest, Portsmouth, Ringwood

NEW FOREST. Mrs J. Pearce, "St Ursula", 30 Hobart Road, New Milton BH25 6EG (01425 613515).
Large detached family home offering every comfort in a friendly relaxed atmosphere. Off Old Milton Road, New Milton. Ideal base for visiting New Forest with its ponies and beautiful walks; Salisbury, Bournemouth easily accessible. Sea one mile. Leisure centre with swimming pool etc, town centre and mainline railway to London minutes away. Twin (en suite), double, family, single rooms, all with handbasin, TV and tea-making facilities. High standards maintained throughout; excellent beds. Two bathrooms/showers, four toilets. Cot etc, available. Pretty garden which guests are welcome to use. Two diningrooms. Smoke detectors installed. Full central heating.

Rates: Bed and Breakfast from £27.50.
• Downstairs twin bedroom suitable for disabled persons. • Children and pets welcome. • Open all year.
ETC ★★★, *NATIONAL ACCESSIBLE SCHEME LEVEL 1.*

Southampton, Winchester

Whether you prefer an active break or a quiet country holiday, Hampshire offers plenty of choices. There are gardens and country parks, historic houses and wildlife parks, museums and castles, and with its location on the Channel coast, all the activities associated with the seaside. Shopping and nightlife, the Historic Dockyard with HMS Victory and the spectacular views of the surrounding area from the Spinnaker Tower, taller even than the London Eye, make Portsmouth well worth a visit. There's plenty to do outdoors in Hampshire. Walking, cycling and horse riding on the heathland and ancient woodlands of the New Forest National Park, and for more thrills, paragliding and hang gliding at the Queen Elizabeth Country Park on the South Downs.

Isle of Wight

All kinds of watersports are available along the coast, but of course the Isle of Wight, only a short ferry ride away from the mainland, is the ultimate destination, with award-winning beaches, water sports centres, seakayaking, diving, sailing and windsurfing. For land-based activities there are over 500 miles of interconnected footpaths, historic castles, dinosaur museums, theme parks and activity centres, while the resorts like Sandown, Shanklin, Ryde and Ventnor offer all that is associated with a traditional seaside holiday. There is a thriving arts community, and of course two internationally renowned music festivals held every year. Something for everyone!

SB

symbols

 　Totally non-smoking　　　　 *Pets Welcome*

 　Children Welcome　　　　　**SB** *Short Breaks available*

 　Suitable for Disabled Guests　 *Licensed*

Ashford, Broadstairs

Kent

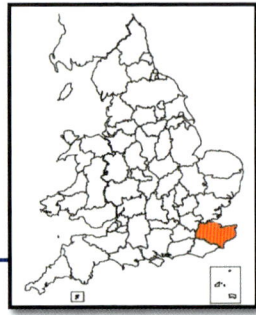

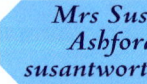

Broadstairs, Canterbury

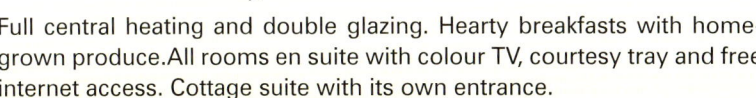

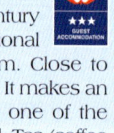

Dover, Folkestone

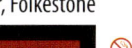

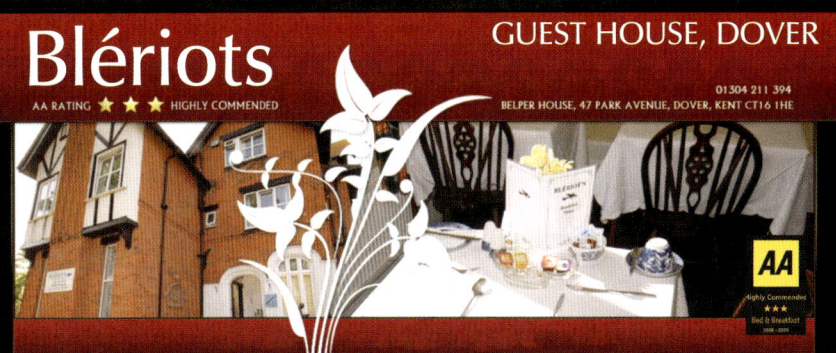

Goudhurst, Hythe, Maidstone

Maidstone

CABBAGES AND KINGS
BED & BREAKFAST

The Old Post Office
Church Road
Halstead
Sevenoaks
Kent TN14 7HE

Surrounded by the peace and quiet of the countryside yet only minutes from the M25, making it superbly well connected for the whole of Kent and Sussex, Gatwick Airport, London and the Channel Tunnel.
Two double bedrooms and one twin room, each en suite and individually designed to a high standard. This beautiful Georgian flint house offers a comfortable blend of old and new, creating a warm, relaxed atmosphere. Traditional English breakfast, vegetarian or seasonal specials.

01959 533054/07773 103578 • jane.whitby@cabbages-and-kings.co.uk • www.cabbages-and-kings.co.uk

SB

Collina House Hotel
East Hill, Tenterden, Kent TN30 6RL
Tel: 01580 764852/764004 • Fax: 01580 762224
www.collinahousehotel.co.uk
e-mail: enquiries@collinahousehotel.co.uk

This charming hotel is quietly situated in the country town of Tenterden, yet is only a few minutes' walk from the Town Centre. There are many National Trust properties and places of interest in the area, including Sissinghurst Castle, Leeds Castle, Scotney Castle Gardens and the Kent and East Sussex steam engines. Personal attention is assured by the Swiss-trained owners of this comfortable hotel, who provide home cooking of the highest standard, enhanced by the use of home-grown produce. All the well-appointed bedrooms, including five family rooms, have private bathrooms, central heating, colour television, direct-dial telephones, tea-making facilities, and hairdryers. Further details on request.

Banbury, Bicester

Oxfordshire

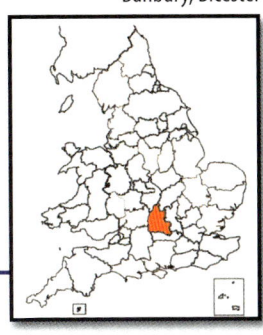

Oxford, the 'city of dreaming spires', has attracted visitors for centuries, and in contrast to lively city life, the Oxfordshire countryside is ideal for a relaxing break. Stretching from Oxford to the Cotswolds, the mysterious Vale of the White Horse is named after the oldest chalk figure in Britain, dating back over 3000 years. Open downland is covered by a network of footpaths connecting up with the ancient Ridgeway Trail and the riverside walks of the Thames Path, or try fishing or boating on the River Thames. The historic market towns like Abingdon and Wantage make good shopping destinations, or visit the pretty villages, stopping for lunch in one of the many traditional English pubs. Follow the village trail at Kidlington, the largest village in England, or visit the nature reserve at Adderbury Lakes, there's always something different to do.

Long Hanborough, Minster Lovell, Oxford

Woodstock

SB

- Beautifully restored 16th century home.
- High priority to cleanliness and quality.
- Large en suite rooms.
- Banquet breakfast using fresh local produce, homemade jams and bread.
- Many super walks including Roman Villa. Close to Blenheim Palace, all Cotswold towns and villages and Oxford City.
- Open all year.
- Two double en suite bedrooms.

B&B from £48-£70 single, £70-£72 double.

Surrey

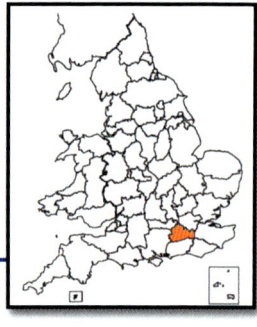

Godalming

GODALMING. Mrs Langdale, Heath Hall Farm, Bowlhead Green, Godalming GU8 6NW (01428 682808).
Converted stable courtyard surrounded by its own farmland on edge of village of Bowlhead Green. Countryside charming with outstanding walking. Ideal base for many famous historic attractions - Loseley House, Petworth House, Wisley RHS Garden, Arundel Castle, Midhurst (Cowdray Castle), historic Portsmouth. Plenty in locality to visit with children. Central for golf courses; polo at Midhurst. Close to South and North Downs. Relaxed atmosphere in house, domestic pets, cattle, sheep, ducks and chooks. All rooms have en suite bathrooms, Freeview TV, tea/coffee making facilities. Wire-free computer access, security encrypted. Three rooms on ground floor. Guests' sitting room with fridge and microwave oven. Ample car parking. Warm welcome with friendly help and advice.
Rates: £35 single room (£40 if one night only), £65 double (£70 if one night only), £80 family room (£90 pne night only), £10 per child (up to 12 years), £15 per child (13 years and over). Cot provided on application (£10 per night).
- Dogs welcome if kept under control and with prior arrangement (£5 per dog per night) • Children welcome
- Open all year • Cards accepted
e-mail: heathhallfarm@btinternet.com   www.heathhallfarm.co.uk

The COMPASSES *Inn*
Purveyors of fine food, ale and .....music!

This attractive inn was once known as the 'God Encompasses' but through time and mispronunciation is now simply known as the 'Compasses'.

Known for its appetising selection of home-cooked dishes and supporting local Surrey Hills Brewery, this friendly hostelry has a warm ambience accentuated by its exposed oak beams and horse brasses.

There is good traditional home-cooked food in the bar and the restaurant. Live music from 9pm every Friday. Situated beneath the North Downs, there is a popular beer garden through which runs the Tillingbourne Stream.

Station Road, Gomshall, Surrey GU5 9LA
Tel: 01483 202 506
www.thecompassesinn.co.uk

SB

The Lawn Guest House
"Everything for the Gatwick Airport Traveller"

Imposing Victorian house set in pretty gardens.
Five minutes by car from Gatwick airport and only 2 minutes walk to the centre of Horley. Main line rail station is 300 yards; London (Victoria) 40 minutes. Comfortable en suite bedrooms, some with both bath and shower; TV, hairdryers, tea/coffee/chocolate trays, d/d phones, computer modem sockets and fully adjustable central heating. Full English or Continental breakfast available. Residents' on-line computer. Overnight parking. Long term parking and airport transfers by arrangement.

SB

30 Massetts Road, Horley, Surrey RH6 7DF
Tel: 01293 775751
Fax: 01293 821803
info@lawnguesthouse.co.uk
www.lawnguesthouse.co.uk

Twin/Double £60 per room • Triple £70 per room, Family room for 4, £80 per room • Family room for 5, £85. All inclusive of English breakfast and tax.

Kingston Upon Thames, Lingfield, Merstham

Less than an hour from London, Surrey is the ideal destination for a day out or short break in the countryside. The most wooded county in the UK, an extensive network of footpaths for walkers covers the chalk downs, woods and heathland of the Surrey Hills and North Downs. Alternatively wander through the traditional villages and historic market towns where there are still many small independent shops to attract you, and stop for lunch at a traditional pub or restaurant. There is a more level walk along the Thames towpath to Runnymeade Meadow where the Magna Carta was signed in 1215, and beside the Wey Navigation Canal, or take a leisurely boat trip through the traditional English countryside. Families will enjoy a visit to a working farm, cycling or horse riding, or for more excitement, try the thrilling rides at one of the theme parks.

Brighton

East Sussex

Rye

Situated in a quiet road, just ten minutes' walk from the centre of medieval Rye, Little Saltcote is an Edwardian family home which offers off-road parking and four comfortable rooms (one at ground floor), all with TV/DVD, radio and beverage tray. We welcome families and are pleased to offer tourist advice or arrange bike hire. Ideally located for touring Sussex and Kent's varied attractions, including everything from sandy beaches to castles, historic houses and gardens. Rates include acclaimed full English or vegetarian breakfast. B&B from £35 per person. Pets welcome by arrangement. No smoking.

Barbara and Denys Martin,
LITTLE SALTCOTE
22 Military Road, Rye TN31 7NY
01797 223210 • Fax: 01797 224474
e-mail: info@littlesaltcote.co.uk • www.littlesaltcote.co.uk

West Sussex

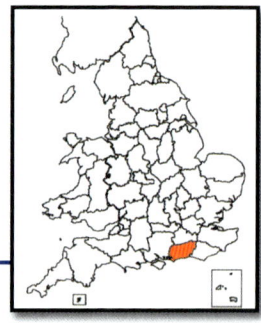

Arundel

SB

• Woodacre •

offers Bed and Breakfast in a traditional family home with accommodation for up to 10-12 guests. The house is set in a beautiful garden surrounded by woodland. We are well positioned for Chichester, Arundel, Goodwood and the seaside and easily accessible from the A27. Our rooms are clean and spacious and two are on the ground floor. We serve a full English breakfast in our conservatory or diningroom overlooking the garden. Plenty of parking space. Everyone is very welcome.

Credit cards accepted.

Mrs Vicki Richards,
Woodacre, Arundel Road,
Fontwell, Arundel BN18 0QP
Tel: 01243 814301
e-mail: wacrebb@aol.com
www.woodacre.co.uk

Bed and Breakfast from £30.00 per person.
3 nights for the price of 2 November to March.

Selsey

SB

ST ANDREWS LODGE

Chichester Road, Selsey, West Sussex PO20 0LX
Tel: 01243 606899 • Fax: 01243 607826

Welcome to St Andrews Lodge, the perfect place for a relaxing break. Situated in the small seaside town of Selsey and well located for Chichester and the South Downs; close to unspoilt beaches and 5 minutes from Pagham Harbour Nature Reserve. Enjoy our delicious breakfast and stay in one of our individually decorated rooms. All rooms have hospitality tray and ironing facilities. Fridges in some of the rooms. Some rooms open on to our large garden to allow your dog to stretch his legs. No charge for dogs but donation to local nature reserve welcome. Licensed bar, wheelchair accessible room, large car park.

*Please apply for brochure and details
of our special winter offer.*

info@standrewslodge.co.uk
www.standrewslodge.co.uk

West and East Sussex share with neighbouring Kent an attractive coastline with cliffs and sandy beaches, and the countryside of the High Weald and the North Downs. There are endless possibilities for outdoor pursuits – walking, cycling, horse riding, golf, and if you're looking for something more adventurous, hang gliding and paragliding! Don't forget the castles, like Bodiam, near Hastings, now restored and run by the National Trust, and the historic ruins at Pevensey and Lewes, or Arundel, one of England's most important stately homes, in West Sussex. If you're looking for beaches, the 100 miles of coast offer something for everyone, whether your preference is for action-packed family fun or a quiet, remote spot. The best known resort is Brighton, with its pebble beach, classic pier, Royal Pavilion and Regency architecture. For a shopping day out visit the designer shops, art galleries and antique shops, or for something different, shop in The Lanes, there's so much to choose from.

The FHG Directory of Website Addresses
on pages 375-392 is a useful quick reference guide for
holiday accommodation with e-mail and/or website details

Cambridge

Cambridgeshire

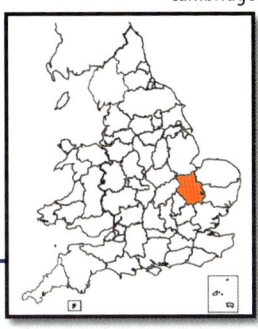

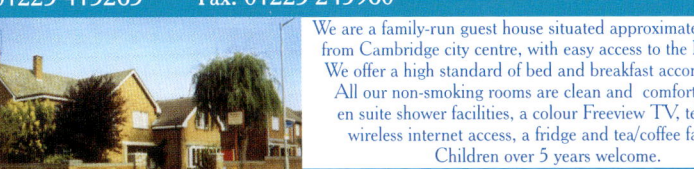

Chelmsford, Colchester

Essex

Kelvedon

Hertfordshire

Much Hadham

Tall Trees

6 Swallow Close
Nightingale Road
Rickmansworth
WD3 7DZ

Large detached house situated in a quiet cul-de-sac with the centre of Rickmansworth only a short walk away. It is a small picturesque old town where there are many places to eat. We are five minutes' walk from the Underground station, half-an-hour to central London. Convenient for M25 and Watford.

Full breakfast served with homemade bread and preserves. Vegetarians and coeliacs catered for.

Tea and coffee making facilities in rooms. Off-street parking. No pets. This is a non-smoking household.

Bed and Breakfast from £33.

Mrs Elizabeth Childerhouse - 01923 720069

Norfolk

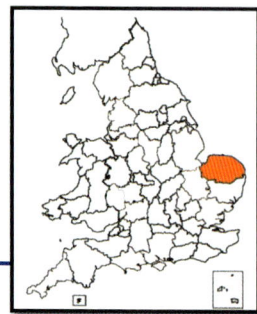

THE OLD PUMP HOUSE

Holman Road, Aylsham, Norwich NR11 6BY
Tel: 01263 733789
theoldpumphouse@btconnect.com
www.theoldpumphouse.com

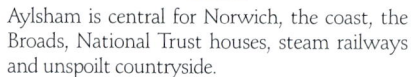

This comfortable 1750s house, owned by Marc James and Charles Kirkman, faces the old thatched pump and is a minute from Aylsham's church and historic marketplace.

It offers five bedrooms (including one four-poster and two family rooms) in a relaxed and elegant setting, with colour TV, tea/coffee making facilities, hairdryers and CD radio alarm clocks in all rooms. Wireless internet access in all rooms.

English breakfast with free-range eggs and local produce (or vegetarian breakfast) is served in the pine-shuttered sitting room overlooking the peaceful garden.

Aylsham is central for Norwich, the coast, the Broads, National Trust houses, steam railways and unspoilt countryside.

• Well behaved children and dogs welcome.
• Dinner by prior arrangement from October to May.
• Non-smoking.
• Off-road parking for six cars.
• *B&B from £75 single, £95 double/twin.*

Along the Norfolk coast from King's Lynn to Great Yarmouth the broad, sandy beaches, grassy dunes, nature reserves, windmills, and pretty little fishing villages are inviting at all times of year. An important trade and fishing port from medieval times, the historic centre of King's Lynn is well worth a visit, and take a break at Great Yarmouth for family entertainment, 15 miles of sandy beaches, traditional piers, a sea life centre and nightlife with clubs and a casino. On the low-lying Fens, the Norfolk Broads or through the ancient pine forests and heathland of The Breck there are walking, cycling and horse riding trails, and market towns and villages to explore. In contrast to the quiet and calm of coast and country, in the medieval city of Norwich with its historic streets and half-timbered houses, cathedral, Norman castle and museums you'll find not only history, but opera, ballet, theatre, music and restaurants .

SB

SB

Mundesley-on-Sea, North Walsham

symbols

 Totally non-smoking   *Pets Welcome*

 Children Welcome   **SB** *Short Breaks available*

 Suitable for Disabled Guests   *Licensed*

Wroxham, Wymondham

WROXHAM. Wroxham Park Lodge, 142 Norwich Road, Wroxham NR12 8SA (01603 782991).

Friendly Bed and Breakfast in an elegant Victorian house, in Wroxham 'Capital of the Norfolk Broads'. Ideal for touring, day boats and boat trips on the beautiful Broads, fishing, steam railways, National Trust Houses, Wroxham Barns. Near north Norfolk coast, Great Yarmouth and Norwich. Good local restaurants and pubs. Guests arriving by train can be met. All rooms en suite, tea/coffee, colour TV. Hearty breakfasts. Large garden, car park, central heating and public telephone.

SB

Rates: Bed and Breakfast from £31 per person.
• Non-smoking • Open all year
VisitBritain ★★★★.
www.wroxhamparklodge.com

Home Farm

Comfortable accommodation set in four acres, quiet location, secluded garden. Conveniently situated off A11 between Attleborough and Wymondham, an excellent location for Snetterton and only 20 minutes from Norwich and 45 minutes from the Norfolk Broads.
Accommodation comprises two double rooms and one single-bedded room, all with TV, tea/coffee facilities and central heating. Children over five years old welcome, but sorry no animals and no smoking. Fishing lakes only ½ mile away.

Bed and Breakfast from £28pppn.

Mrs Joy Morter, Home Farm,
Morley, Wymondham NR18 9SU
Tel: 01953 602581

Bungay

Suffolk

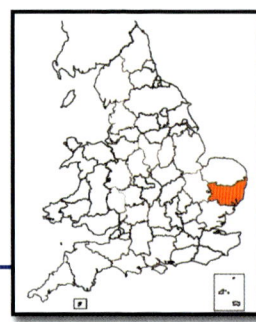

SB

Earsham Park Farm

Bed and breakfast in rural East Anglia

Luxury bed and breakfast accommodation in a comfortable and informal Victorian farmhouse with sweeping views over the Waveney Valley. Earsham Park Farm is situated 3 miles from Bungay and only 5 miles from Harleston. Within easy driving distance are the historic city of Norwich, the seaside town of Southwold, the extensive waterways of the Norfolk Broads and the Norfolk and Suffolk coastal resorts.

Enormous care has been taken to completely refurbish the house yet retain the elegance and charm of the Victorian era and combine it with every modern comfort and convenience. The atmosphere is relaxed and informal with three elegant and spacious en suite guest rooms, each with its own character and beautiful furnishings.

01986 892180
earshamparkfarm@googlemail.com
www.earsham-parkfarm.co.uk
Old Railway Road, Earsham,
Bungay NR35 2AQ

AA
★★★★
FARMHOUSE

Green Tourism
SILVER

Gold AWARD

enjoyEngland.com
★★★★
FARMHOUSE

Suffolk's 40 miles of unspoilt World Heritage coastline is perfect for a seaside holiday. Wander through the coastal forests or along the shingle and sandy beaches admiring the scenery, or hire bicycles for a family bike ride. Eat oysters at Orford or follow the Suffolk Coastal Churches Trail. Fishing is particularly popular on the Waveney as well as many on other rivers and golfers have a choice of short local courses and some of championship standard. Horse racing enthusiasts can't miss Newmarket, whether for a fun day out, to visit the National Horseracing Museum or to take a guided tour round the National Stud. However you choose to spend the day, the wonderful choice of locally produced food served in one of the many pubs, restaurants and cafes will provide the perfect end to your stay.

Bury St Edmunds

Readers are requested to mention this FHG guide when seeking accommodation

Please note...

All the information in this book is given in good faith in the belief that it is correct. However, the publishers cannot guarantee the facts given in these pages, neither are they responsible for changes in policy, ownership or terms that may take place after the date of going to press. Readers should always satisfy themselves that the facilities they require are available and that the terms, if quoted, still apply.

Hopton, Ipswich

The Old Rectory is a Listed building dating from the 16th century, well situated to explore East Anglia, being on the Suffolk/Norfolk border. Bury St Edmunds is 12 miles away, the market town of Diss is 8. Cambridge, Ipswich and Norwich are within easy reach. The house is beautifully furnished and many period features add to the charm of this lovely stylish family home.
Sarah and Bobby delight in entertaining guests in their beautifully restored home.

- 2 double bedded rooms en suite • Twin bedded room en suite
- Continental/English Breakfast
- Dinner available by arrangement. • Licensed
- Children welcome by arrangement
- Dogs welcome by arrangement (extra £10.00)
- Drawing Room with unique rotunda • Next to church
- No smoking house • Large garden • Croquet
- Closed Christmas, New Year and occasionally at other times.
- Credit/debit cards not accepted

**Bobby & Sarah Llewellyn, The Old Rectory
Hopton, Suffolk IP22 2QX • Tel: 01953 688135
e-mail: llewellyn.hopton@btinternet.com
www.theoldrectoryhopton.com**

High View

A comfortable modernised Edwardian house set in a large secluded garden located four miles south of Ipswich. Ideally situated to explore the Suffolk Heritage Coast and countryside, within easy reach of "Constable Country", Lavenham, Kersey, the historic market town of Bury St Edmunds plus many other picturesque locations.

twin, double and single bedrooms • guests' bathroom with shower and toilet • lounge with TV • good pub meals available in the village. From £27 per person per night • No smoking.

**Mrs Rosanna Steward, High View,
Back Lane, Washbrook, Ipswich IP8 3JA
Tel: 01473 730494**
e-mail: rosanna3@suffolkholidays.com • www.suffolkholidays.com

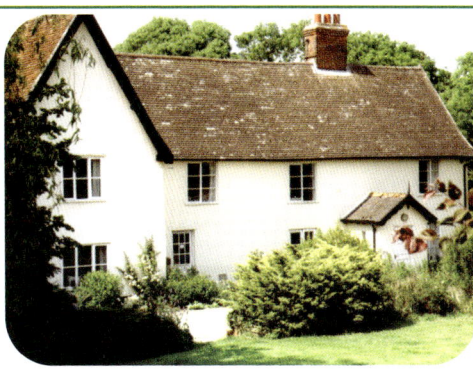

Sweffling Hall Farm

Set well back from the main Framlingham-Saxmundham road, in a quiet location with pond and garden. We have chickens providing free-range eggs. Convenient for Woodland Trust (nearby), Framlingham Castle, Saxstead Mill and Coast. Only 9 miles away is Aldeburgh and Minsmere Bird Reserve. Ideal for walking and cycling; vintage transport can be provided free for those staying longer. Two double rooms with private/en suite bathroom and a family room with one double bed and two single beds. There is also a garden with a large pond that can be viewed from the family room.

SB

SWEFFLING HALL FARM

Sweffling, Saxmundham IP17 2BT
Tel & Fax: 01728 663644
e-mail: stephen.mann@unicombox.com
www.swefflinghallfarm.co.uk

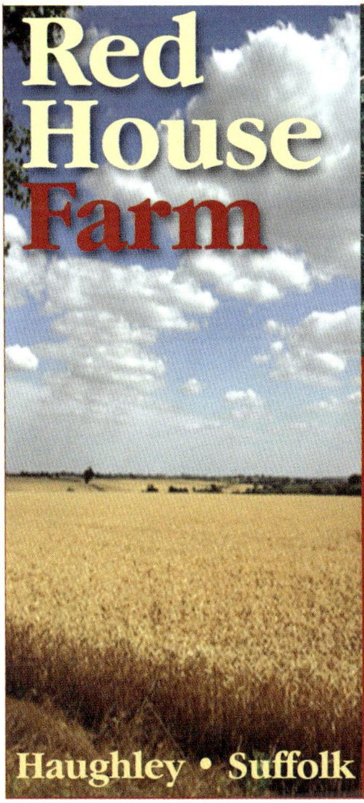

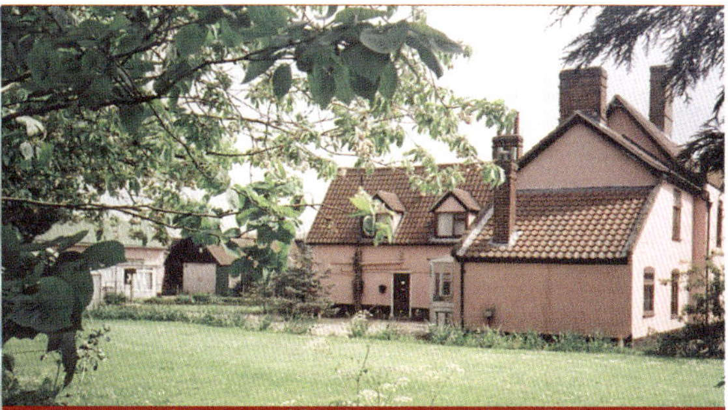

SB

A warm welcome and homely atmosphere awaits you at our attractive farmhouse set in the beautiful surroundings of mid-Suffolk. Comfortably furnished bedrooms with en suite shower rooms, tea/coffee making facilities. One double, one twin and two single rooms. Central heating. Guests' own lounge with TV; dining room. Ideal location for exploring, walking, cycling and birdwatching.

Open all year • No smoking • No pets
B&B from £65-£70 per double/twin room;
£40 to £45 per single room.

Mrs Mary Noy, Red House Farm, Station Road, Haughley, Near Stowmarket IP14 3QP
Tel: 01449 673323 • Fax: 01449 675413
e-mail: mary@redhousefarmhaughley.co.uk
www.redhousefarmhaughley.co.uk

Woodbridge/Framlingham

The FHG Directory of Website Addresses
on pages 375-392 is a useful quick reference guide for
holiday accommodation with e-mail and/or website details

Ashbourne

Derbyshire

Guests are warmly welcomed into the friendly atmosphere of Braemar, situated in a quiet residential part of this famous spa town. Within five minutes' walk of all the town's many and varied attractions:

Pavilion Gardens, Opera House, swimming pool; golf courses, horse riding, walking, fishing, etc are all within easy reach in this area renowned for its scenic beauty. Many of the Peak District's famous beauty spots including Chatsworth, Haddon Hall, Bakewell, Matlock, Dovedale and Castleton are nearby.

Accommodation comprises comfortable double and twin bedded rooms fully en suite with colour TV and hospitality trays. Wi-Fi available. Full English Breakfast served and diets catered for. Non-smokers preferred.

Terms from £27.50 inclusive for Bed and Breakfast. Weekly terms available.

Braemar

Roger and Maria Hyde
10 Compton Road, Buxton SK17 9DN
Tel: 01298 78050 • e-mail: buxtonbraemar@supanet.com
www.cressbrook.co.uk/buxton/braemar

Causeway House
B&B

**Back Street, Castleton,
Hope Valley S33 8WE
01433 623291**
email: info@causewayhouse.co.uk
www.causewayhouse.co.uk

Causeway House is a 14th Century Cruck Cottage in the heart of Castleton in the beautiful Peak District. The area is renowned for its scenery, history and heritage with amazing walks, cycling and Blue John caves to visit.

The accommodation has three en suite double rooms, a single and a twin room with shared bathroom. One of the rooms has a four-poster bed.

Nick and Janet Steynberg offer you a hearty Full English, Continental or Vegetarian Breakfast.
A piece of Heaven for you and your family.

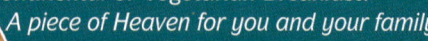

For walking, climbing, mountain biking and caving visit Derbyshire. There are activities available at every level and courses to suit everyone. From the gently rolling farmland and National Forest in the south to the rugged demanding landscape of the Dark Peak in the north there are trails for cyclists and walkers to follow, many along old railway lines. Everyone can visit Poole's Cavern to see the best stalagmites and stalactites in Derbyshire (and discover the difference!), and the Blue John Cave at Castleton where this rare mineral is mined, and perhaps buy a sample of jewellery in one of the local shops. Buxton was a spa from Roman times, but the main attractions now are concerts, theatre and the annual literary and music festival. Concerts are held at Calke Abbey and at Chatsworth, the best known of the stately homes, with impressive interiors and magnificent gardens and grounds, and period dramas at Haddon Hall at Bakewell.

BONEHILL FARM

01332 513553

This 120 acre mixed farm with Georgian farmhouse is set in peaceful rural surroundings, yet offers all the convenience of being only three miles west of Derby, on the A516 between Mickleover and Etwall. Within 10 miles there is a choice of historic houses to visit; Calke Abbey, Kedleston Hall, Sudbury Hall. Peak District 20 miles, Alton Towers 20 miles.

Accommodation in three bedrooms (one twin, one double en suite, one family room with en suite facilities), all with tea/coffee making facilities. Cot and high chair provided. Open all year. Croquet available.

B&B per night: single from £30, double from £55.

A warm and friendly welcome awaits you.

Mrs Catherine Dicken, Bonehill Farm, Etwall Road, Mickleover DE3 0DN
e-mail: bonehillfarm@hotmail.com   www.bonehillfarm.co.uk

SB

Graham and Julie Caesar
Windy Harbour Farm Hotel
Woodhead Road, Glossop SK13 7QE
01457 853107 • www.peakdistrict-hotel.co.uk

Situated in the heart of the Peak District on the B6105, approximately one mile from Glossop town centre and adjacent to the Pennine Way.

All our bedrooms are en suite, with outstanding views of Woodhead and Snake Passes and the Longdendale Valley is an ideal location for all outdoor activities.

A warm welcome awaits you in our licensed bar and restaurant serving a wide range of excellent home-made food.

Bed and Breakfast from £30 per night

Stanton-by-Bridge, Winster

Hereford, Ledbury

Herefordshire

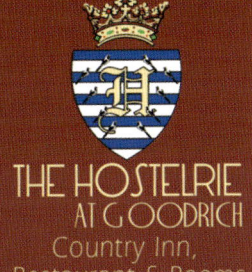

SB

Thatch Close Farm
Bed & Breakfast
Llangrove, Ross-on-Wye HR9 6EL

Situated between the Wye Valley and the Forest of Dean, with marvellous views from every angle, yet convenient for A40, M4 and M50, Thatch Close is the ideal location for a weekend break or a longer stay.

Our home offers a warm welcome to travellers, walkers, fishermen, and tourists. We take pride in making you feel at home, from the moment of your arrival and throughout your stay.

Thatch Close is ideally situated for exploration of one of the most historically rich and rewarding parts of Britain, with easy access to the Wye Valley, the Forest of Dean, the Border Castles, Hay-on-Wye, the Brecon Beacons, Hereford Cathedral and the Mappa Mundi, Offa's Dyke and the medieval town of Monmouth.

Our three lovely bedrooms, all en suite, have magnificent views over the unspoilt countryside. Relax in the visitors' lounge or sit in the shade of mature trees in our garden. You may be greeted by our dog or free-flying parrot. Children and dogs are welcome.
Terms from £60 per room.
Please telephone or e-mail for brochure.

**Wildlife Action
Gold Award**

Mrs M.E. Drzymalski
Tel: 01989 770300

e-mail: info@thatchclose.co.uk
www.thatchclose.co.uk

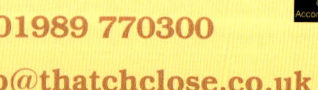
AA
★★★★
Guest
Accommodation

Ross-on-Wye

Leicestershire & Rutland

Belton-in-Rutland

Please note...

All the information in this book is given in good faith in the belief that it is correct. However, the publishers cannot guarantee the facts given in these pages, neither are they responsible for changes in policy, ownership or terms that may take place after the date of going to press. Readers should always satisfy themselves that the facilities they require are available and that the terms, if quoted, still apply.

Melton Mowbray

Set in the centre of the Midlands, the rolling countryside, canals, forests, beautiful villages, interesting market towns and history make Leicestershire and Rutland well worth a visit. Spend a peaceful hour or two cruising along the Ashby Canal in a narrowboat past Bosworth Battlefield where the Wars of the Roses ended in 1485. With over 1000 different species there's plenty to see at Twycross Zoo at Hinckley, or take a walk through Burbage Wood to see the native fauna. Wander along the banks of the River Soar at the conservation village of Blaby, or in summer try to find the way round the Maize Maze at Wistow. Rutland is England's smallest county with the largest man-made lake in Europe. Cycle round the shoreline, cruise on the water, walk round the lake, while the really energetic can take the walkers' route, Round Rutland, all of 65 miles long.

symbols

 Totally non-smoking

 Children Welcome

 Suitable for Disabled Guests

 Pets Welcome

 *Short Breaks available*

 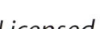 *Licensed*

Lincolnshire

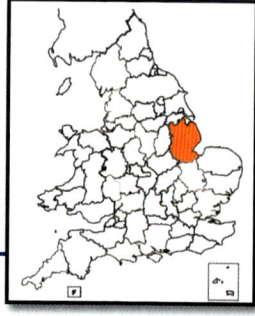

We welcome you to our small, friendly, family-run farmhouse in the delightful hamlet of Deepdale, to enjoy the comfort of our home and garden. Our rooms have en suite or private bathroom, tea/coffee making facilities, TV, radio and hairdryer. Trouser press, iron and board, wet outdoor clothes drying facilities available. We offer the 'Great British' breakfast, with fresh, locally sourced produce where possible; vegetarian and other diets as requested.
We are central for visiting Hull, Beverley, Lincoln and York, and close to historic Barton. There is a SSSI, 3 miles away on the Humber Estuary, and we are 200 yards from a bridleway, leading to a network of bridleways and the Viking Way.
Dogs and horses welcome by arrangement. We have plenty of off-road parking.

Terms from £24.00 pppn. Special breaks and long term discounts available.

NO SMOKING

Mrs. Pam Atkin
West Wold Farmhouse
Deepdale
Barton-upon-Humber
DN18 6ED
Tel: 01652 633293 / 07889 532937
e-mail: pam@westwoldfarmhouse.co.uk
www.westwoldfarmhouse.co.uk

Coast or country, the choice is yours for a holiday in Lincolnshire. With award-winning beaches, miles of clean sand, theme parks, kite surfing, wake boarding and water skiing, there's action and excitement for everyone along the Fun Coast and at Cleethorpes on the Humber estuary. At Skegness, as well as all the fun on the beach, children will love watching the seals being fed at the seal sanctuary, and the exotic birds and butterflies flying overhead in the tropical house. Further north, at Cleethorpes with its wonderful beaches, take a ride on the Cleethorpes Coast Light Railway. Keen fishermen can always find a peaceful spot along the extensive network of rivers and canals and for golfers there's a wide variety and standard of courses, with the home of amateur golf in England at the National Golf Centre at Woodhall Spa. In Lincoln walk round the battlements at the Castle, explore the cobbled streets lined with medieval buildings and visit the imposing Gothic cathedral, one of the finest in Europe. Cruise on the Roman canal that flows through the city, shop at the boutiques, eat at the restaurants and cafes, and in the evening enjoy a concert or a visit to the theatre.

An early 18th century Listed farmhouse with spacious en suite bedrooms and original beamed ceilings.

Enjoy a generous farmhouse breakfast using fresh local produce.

Centrally located for five 'Bomber Country' museums, championship golf at Woodhall Spa, antiques at Horncastle and local fishing. Historic pubs nearby serving excellent evening meals. Within easy reach of the east coast and the Lincolnshire Wolds.

• •One double and one twin bedroom• •
• •Central heating, tea and coffee facilities and colour TV• •

Open all year except Christmas • No smoking
Children welcome • B&B from £20pp.

Mrs C. Whittington, High House Farm, Tumby Moorside, Near Coningsby, Boston PE22 7ST • Tel: 01526 345408
e-mail: HighHousefarm@aol.com
www.high-house-farm.co.uk

The Black Swan Guest House

21 High Street, Marton, Gainsborough, Lincs DN21 5AH
Tel: 01427 718878
info@blackswanguesthouse.co.uk • www.blackswanguesthouse.co.uk

As resident proprietors, Judy and John Patrick offer a warm welcome at our delightfully converted former 18th century coaching inn. The property has been fully refurbished, using much of the original materials and retaining many original features.

The house and stable block now offer comfortable rooms which are en suite, with digital TV and tea/coffee making facilities. There is a guest lounge where you can enjoy a drink in the evenings, or just relax. Our breakfasts are all freshly cooked to order using locally sourced best quality produce.

The local area is steeped in history, from Roman times through to the old airfields of the Second World War, and the city of Lincoln is only 12 miles away, with its stunning cathedral and old city centre in the Bailgate area. For those of you who need to keep in touch, wireless broadband is available.

We are a non-smoking establishment.

Single from £45, double/twin from £68.

SB

AA
★★★★
Guest
Accommodation

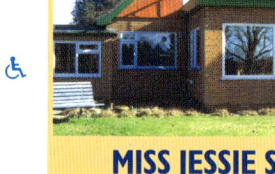
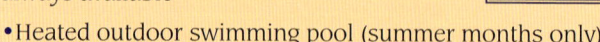

Market Rasen, Peterborough

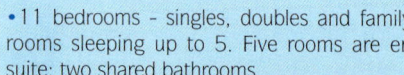

symbols

 Totally non-smoking

 Children Welcome

 Suitable for Disabled Guests

 Pets Welcome

 SB *Short Breaks available*

 Licensed

Kettering

Northamptonshire

ENJOY A HOLIDAY in our comfortable 17th century farmhouse with oak beams and inglenook fireplaces. Four-poster bed now available. Peaceful surroundings, large garden containing ancient circular dovecote. Dairy Farm is a working farm situated in a beautiful Northamptonshire village just off the A14, within easy reach of many places of interest or ideal for a restful holiday. Good farmhouse food and friendly atmosphere. Open all year, except Christmas.
B&B from £27 to £38 (children under 10 half price); Evening Meal £17.

enjoyEngland.com

★★★
FARMHOUSE

Mrs A. Clarke
Dairy Farm
Cranford St Andrew
Kettering NN14 4AQ
Tel: 01536 330273

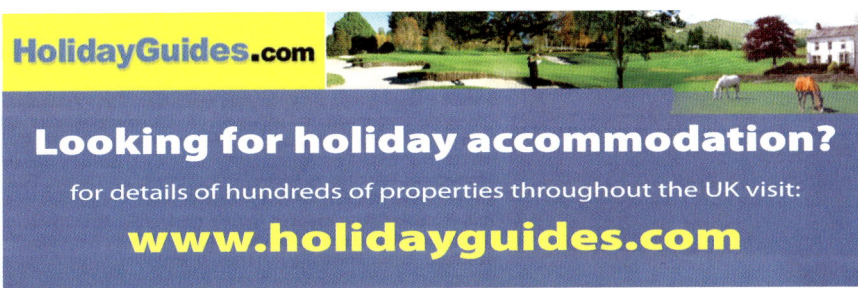

Long Buckby

Nottinghamshire

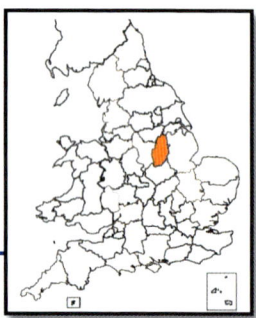

Burton Joyce

BURTON JOYCE. Mrs V. Baker, Willow House, Burton Joyce, Nottingham NG14 5FD (0115 931 2070; Mob: 07816 347706).
A period house (1857) in quiet village two minutes' walk from beautiful river bank, yet only five miles from City. Attractive, interesting accommodation with authentic Victorian ambience. En suite available. Bright, clean rooms with tea/coffee facilities, TV. Off-road parking. Porch for smokers. Ideally situated for Holme Pierrepont International Watersports Centre; golf; National Ice Centre; Trent Bridge (cricket); Sherwood Forest; Nottingham Racecourse; Shelford Pony Trials and the unspoiled historic town of Southwell with its Minster and Racecourse. Good local eating. Please phone first for directions. *Rates: From £26 per person per night.*
website: www.willowhousebedandbreakfast.co.uk

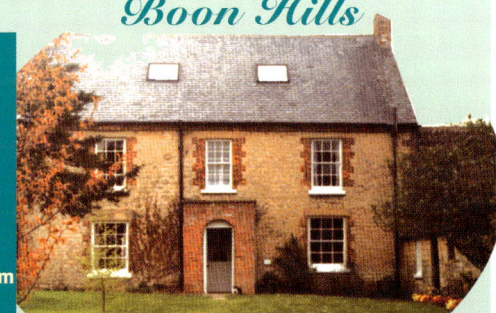

Nottinghamshire's historic and literary connections make it a highly interesting area to spend a short break or longer holiday. Myth, legend and fact all play a part in the stories of Robin Hood, but visit Sherwood Forest, the hiding place of outlaws in medieval times, and make up your own mind from the evidence you find there. Whether you prefer taking part in sport or just enjoy watching, there's a great variety available. Watch cricket at Trent Bridge, horse racing at Nottingham and the all-weather course at Southwell, and ice hockey at Nottingham's National Ice Centre, or try ice skating yourself. There are golf courses from municipal and pay & play to championship standard, fishing in canals, lakes and fisheries, and everyone is welcome to play at the Nottingham Tennis Centre. The city of Nottingham is a wonderful place to shop, with designer outlets, independent shops and department stores, and don't miss the traditional Lace Market.

Shropshire

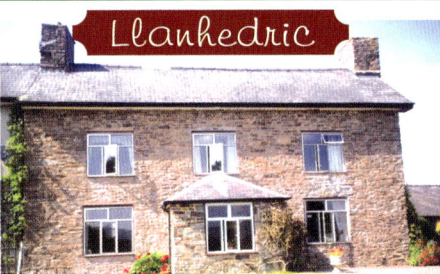

If you're looking for a break from the pace of life today, but with plenty to do and see, and with a choice of superb food to round off your day, Shropshire is the place to visit. Visit the Shropshire Hills Discovery Centre at Craven Arms, where you can take a simulated balloon ride and meet the Shropshire mammoth. Stokesay Castle, the finest 13th century fortified manor house in England, is just one of over 30 castles in the county, as well as stately homes and all kinds of gardens, including Hawkstone Historic Park and Follies, a fairytale kingdom near Shrewsbury. At the Ironbridge Gorge museums, as well as learning all about the early inventions leading to the start of the Industrial Revolution, discover how all kinds of present-day objects work – and make it happen yourself.

The Mill House
Shrewsbury Road, High Ercall, Telford TF6 6BE

Judy and Chris Yates welcome you to The Mill House, an 18th century converted water mill situated beside the River Roden on a 9 acre working small holding. Located in the village of High Ercall, halfway between the historic county town of Shrewsbury and the new town of Telford.

Luxury B&B accommodation in three beautifully decorated, en suite bedrooms. Perfect for exploring Shropshire and the Welsh borderlands. A short distance from the World Heritage Site of the Ironbridge Gorge and the surrounding area offers a wide range of attractions and activities to suit all tastes.

Children welcome. Dogs by prior arrangement. Non-smoking.
Single £39 pppn. Double/Twin £28pppn.
Family room (sleeps 4) from £24 pppn.

Tel: 01952 770394
e-mail: cjpy@lineone.net
www.ercallmill.co.uk

Alton

Staffordshire

The Mousehole

A 17thC stone cottage with original features but modern amenities. Two double rooms, both en suite with tea/coffee facilities and TV; en suite family suite. Safe parking and garden. Facilities for walkers and cyclists. Open all year. Full English Breakfast. Special diets available on request. Surrounded by the rural beauty of Cotton Dell with acres of woodland, public footpaths for walkers, cycle paths and cycle hire close by.

SB

- Alton Towers within three minutes' drive.
- Good local pubs and restaurants.
- Churnet Valley Railway in steam at weekends.

www.themouseholebandb.co.uk
sales@themouseholebandb.co.uk
01538 703351 • *Keith & Sandra Alcock*
Cotton Lane, Cotton,
Staffordshire Moorlands ST10 3DS

Situated right in the middle of England, Staffordshire is a county of open spaces and ancient woodlands, exciting theme parks, stately homes and castles, miles of canals and the largest street-style skate park in Europe at Stoke-on-Trent. There are thrills and fun for every age group at the theme parks. As well as the heart-stopping rides, walk through the Ocean Tank Tunnel at Alton Towers to watch the sea creatures from all the world's oceans and make a big splash in the Waterpark. Take a look at life in the past at the complete working historic estate at Shugborough near Stafford, with working kitchens, dairy water mill and brewhouse. Out in the open heathland of Cannock Chase in the south there are well maintained paths and trails for all levels of mountain biking, bikes to hire and fishing pools at Rugely and walking and cycling trails at Hednesford, or follow the Chase Heritage Trail.

Cheadle, Eccleshall

SB

Warwickshire

Stratford-Upon-Avon

West Midlands

Wolverhampton

Droitwich Spa

Worcestershire

Worcestershire, stretching south-east from the fringes of Birmingham, is a county of Georgian towns, Cotswold stone villages, Victorian spas, former industrial centres and wonderful walking country. Long distance trails cross the countryside in all directions, like the Geopark Way, over a hundred miles of rock over 700 million years old from Shropshire, to Gloucester. In the Malvern Hills choose between gentle and more strenuous exercise to appreciate the wonderful views of the surrounding countryside. If you're looking for a different kind of challenge, try mountain boarding in the hills near Malvern. Alternatively take a more restful look at the countryside by taking a ride on the Severn Valley Railway between Bromsgrove and Kidderminster. In Malvern there are festivals for music and the arts, and the Malvern Theatres For an unusual museum, go to the Avoncraft Museum of Historic Buildings at Bromsgrove, which houses the national collection of telephone kiosks, and of course there are country mansions and gardens to visit too.

symbols

  Totally non-smoking   Pets Welcome

  Children Welcome   **SB** Short Breaks available

  Suitable for Disabled Guests   Licensed

East Yorkshire

SB

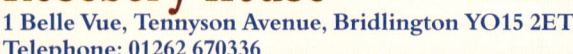

Bridlington

East Yorkshire is all about fun and action outdoors. From building sandcastles on the award-winning beaches along the North Sea coast in the east to walking in the Wolds inland, all the family will find an activity to enjoy. The Blue Flag beaches at Bridlington and Hornsea are ideal for children and if they tire of the sun and sand there's plenty of traditional entertainment too. Water sports aren't confined to the seaside, with windsurfing at Dacre Lakeside Park and jet skiing at Fossehill near Driffield, an ideal centre from which to explore both coast and country, and for golfers there's a choice of clifftop links and parkland courses inland and on the coast. For a taste of city life visit Hull, with its lovely waterfront, explore the Old Town while following the sculptures of the Seven Seas Fish Trail, enjoy modern drama at the Truck Theatre, and jazz, sea shanty and literature festivals, or watch football and rugby at the KC Stadium.

Kilnwick Percy

North Yorkshire

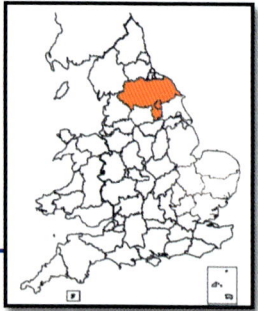

Coverdale

Rowantree Farm

ROWANTREE FARM is a family-run dairy farm situated in the heart of the North York Moors. Ideal walking and mountain biking area, with panoramic moorland views. Coast easily accessible.
Our non-smoking home comprises one family room and one twin-bedded room, with private bathroom and private shower room, also full central heating, beverage tray, CD clock radio and hairdryer. Relax in our residents' lounge with colour TV/video. Ample car parking.

- *Children welcome; cot and high chair available.*
- *Good home cooking (vegetarians catered for), served in our separate dining room.*
- *Packed lunches available.*
- *B&B from £27; Evening Meal by prior arrangement.*

Mrs L. Tindall, Rowantree Farm, Ainthorpe, Whitby YO21 2LE
Tel: 01287 660396 • e-mail: krbsatindall@aol.com
www.rowantreefarm.co.uk

Harrogate

The city of York in North Yorkshire is full of attractions for the visitor. View it gently floating through the air on a balloon trip, or if you prefer to keep your feet on the ground take a walk round the ancient walls, to get a first glimpse of the compact urban centre dominated by the magnificent York Minster, the largest medieval Gothic cathedral in northern Europe. Have fun finding your way through the the Snickelways, the maze of hidden alleyways, and enjoy a morning – or longer – in the interesting independent little shops and boutiques as well as all the top high street stores. Outside the city the vast open stretches of the North York Moors and the Yorkshire Dales National Parks and the golden sandy beaches of the coast are perfect for an active holiday. Walking, riding, cycling, horse riding, or just enjoying the great outdoors, North Yorkshire provides an ideal destination.

Helmsley is beautifully situated for touring the North York Moors National Park, East Coast, York, "Herriot" and "Heartbeat" country. There is a wealth of footpaths and bridleways to explore. A warm welcome awaits you in the comfortable relaxed atmosphere of this elegant Georgian town house just off the market square, overlooking All Saints Church to the front and Helmsley Castle to the rear.

All rooms are en suite, with tea/coffee making facilities, digital colour TV, radio alarm, hairdryer, central heating. Private gardens and car park. Highly recommended for good food. Bed and Breakfast from £28pppn. Please telephone, or write, for colour brochure.

As recommended by the *Which?* Good B&B Guide.

Stilworth House

1 Church Street, Helmsley YO62 5AD

Mrs C. Swift

Tel: 01439 771072 • www.stilworth.co.uk

e-mail: carol@stilworth.co.uk

Barn Close Farm

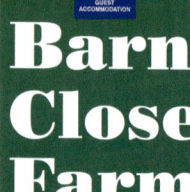

Rievaulx,
Helmsley,
North Yorkshire
YO62 5LH

01439 798321

Mrs J. Milburn

BARN CLOSE FARM is nicely situated in the North York Moors National Park. This family farm in beautiful surroundings offers homely accommodation to holidaymakers all year round. Within easy reach of Rievaulx Abbey and many other places of interest, it is an ideal centre for tourists.

Pony trekking nearby • Good walking terrain!
Highly commended for good food.

Two double rooms, one en suite; bathroom; toilets;
sitting room and dining room.

Bed and Breakfast from £28 to £40, Evening Dinner £18.
"WHICH?" RECOMMENDED. "DAILY TELEGRAPH" RECOMMENDED.

• Brickfields Farm •

Kirkby Mills, Kirkbymoorside YO62 6NS

Stylish, award-winning farmhouse B&B in rural North Yorkshire.

Six light and airy guest rooms in the recently renovated Barn. Quality beds, comfortable seating areas with large sofa, flat screen TV, DVD, Freeview and well-stocked hospitality trays.

Spacious en suite bathrooms feature walk-in "wet room" style showers, heated towel rails and "soft close" toilet seats.

All rooms: ground floor, French doors opening to terrace, easily accessible for the less able guest, wholesome Yorkshire breakfasts.

Wide range of restaurants and dining pubs locally. Brickfields Farm makes an ideal base for exloring North York Moors, Whitby and East coast, the local Abbeys, castles and stately homes.

Ample parking • No Smoking • No Children • No Pets

Janet Trousdale

Tel: 01751 433074

e-mail: janet@brickfieldsfarm.co.uk

www.brickfieldsfarm.co.uk

B&B from £47.50. Open all year.

Outside the city of York the vast open stretches of the North York Moors and the Yorkshire Dales National Parks and the golden sandy beaches of the coast are perfect for an active holiday. Walking, riding, cycling, horse riding, or just enjoying the great outdoors, North Yorkshire provides an ideal destination. Every standard of fitness and ability is catered for, whatever the sport or activity. Walkers will find gentle short circular routes centred on interesting, historic stone villages and busy market towns, and more arduous long distance trails, like the Cleveland Way, the Pennine Trail and the Dales Way, or the really challenging Yorkshire Three Peaks in Ribblesdale.

SB

Malham • Miresfield Farm

★★★
GUEST HOUSE

- In beautiful gardens bordering village green and stream.
- Well known for excellent food.
- 11 bedrooms, all with private facilities.

Mr C. Sharp, Miresfield Farm, Malham, Skipton BD23 4DA • Tel: 01729 830414 www.miresfield-farm.com

- Full central heating.
- Two well furnished lounges and conservatory for guests' use.
- B&B from £32pppn.

Banavie
Bed & Breakfast

Holiday Accommodation in Thornton-Le-Dale, Pickering, Yorkshire

A large semi-detached house set in a quiet part of the picturesque village of Thornton-le-Dale, one of the prettiest villages in Yorkshire with its famous thatched cottage and bubbling stream flowing through the centre.

We offer our guests a quiet night's sleep and rest away from the main road, yet only four minutes' walk from the village centre.

One large double or twin bedroom and two double bedrooms, all tastefully decorated with en suite facilities, colour TV, hairdryer, shaver point etc. and tea/coffee making facilities. There is a large guest lounge, tea tray on arrival. A real Yorkshire breakfast is served in the dining room.

Places to visit include Castle Howard, Eden Camp, North Yorkshire Moors Railway, Goathland ("Heartbeat"), York etc. There are three pubs, a bistro and a fish and chip shop for meals. Children and dogs welcome. Own keys. Car parking at back of house.

B&B from £29 pppn
• SAE please for brochure • Welcome To Excellence
• Hygiene Certificate held • No Smoking
Mrs Ella Bowes

BANAVIE, ROXBY ROAD, THORNTON-LE-DALE, PICKERING YO18 7SX
Tel: 01751 474616
e-mail: info@banavie.uk.com www.banavie.uk.com

Mrs Julie Bailes, CHERRY CROFT, Bedale Lane, Wath, Ripon HG4 5ER

- CHERRY CROFT is situated in the quiet village of Wath, approx. three miles north of the historic market town of Ripon; two miles from A1(M).
- Accommodation comprises two double rooms with TV and tea making facilities.
- All rooms are on the ground floor.
- Ideal location for touring the Dales and Herriot Country.
- £20 per person, Bed & Breakfast.

Tel: 01765 640318

SB

Scarborough •••• *Terrace Hotel*

A small family-run Hotel situated between North and South Bays, close to all Scarborough's many attractions and only a short walk from the town centre, rail and bus stations. Private car park. Three double bedrooms (one en suite), three family rooms (one en suite) and one single bedroom, all with colour TV and tea making facilities. Full Fire Certificate. Totally non-smoking.

Bed and full English Breakfast from £20.00. En suite facilities £3 extra pppn.
One night supplement £2.00 pp.
Children (sharing room with adults) under 4 years FREE, 4 to 13 years half price.

Sylvia and Chris Kirk, The Terrace Hotel, 69 Westborough, Scarborough YO11 1TS • 01723 374937

www.4hotels.co.uk/uk/hotels/theterrace.html • www.smoothhound.co.uk/hotels/theterrace.html

Killerby Cottage Farm

Silver
SILVER AWARD

Simon and Val extend a warm Yorkshire welcome and invite you to share their charming farmhouse in the pleasant countryside between Scarborough and Filey. All our bedrooms are tastefully decorated and have en suite facilities, colour TV, and well-stocked beverage trays. Hearty breakfasts that will keep you going all day are served in the conservatory overlooking the lovely garden.

Our 350-acre farm has diversified and we now have the Stained Glass Centre and tearoom which are open to visitors. Cayton offers easy access to Scarborough, Filey, Whitby, the North York Moors, and York.

Simon and Val Green
Killerby Cottage Farm
Killerby Lane, Cayton, Scarborough YO11 3TP
Tel: 01723 581236 • Fax: 01723 585146
e-mail: val@stainedglasscentre.co.uk
www.smoothhound.co.uk/hotels/killerby

Scarborough, Skipton

Detached 16th century farmhouse in private grounds. Quiet, with safe parking. One mile east of Skipton, Gateway to the Dales, and close to many places of beauty and interest. Luxury B&B with fireside treats in the lounge. All rooms are quiet and spacious, with panoramic views, washbasin and toilet (some full en suite), tea/coffee facilities and electric overblankets.
Sorry, no smoking, no pets, no children.
Terms: £28-£38pppn; single occupancy £38-£56.
Open all year.
Farm cottage sometimes available.

SB

Tel: 01756 793849
www.lowskibeden.co.uk

LOW SKIBEDEN FARMHOUSE, HARROGATE ROAD, SKIPTON BD23 6AB

Situated on a quiet terrace in the old part of the picturesque, historic village of Staithes, with its artistic and Captain Cook associations, Brooklyn is a solid, red brick house, built in 1921 by a retired sea captain. It has three letting rooms (two doubles, one twin) which are individually decorated with views across the rooftops to Cowbar cliffs. All have a television and tea/coffee making facilities, and although not en suite, do have washbasins. The dining room doubles as a sitting room for guests, and breakfasts are generous, vegetarians catered for, and special diets by arrangement. Pets and children are most welcome.

MS M.J. HEALD, BROOKLYN B&B,
BROWN'S TERRACE, STAITHES,
NORTH YORKSHIRE TS13 5BG
Tel: 01947 841396

m.heald@tiscali.co.uk
www.brooklynuk.co.uk

The Gallery Bed & Breakfast

The Gallery is ideally located in the old market town of Thirsk in North Yorkshire, perfect for short breaks exploring the Yorkshire Dales and the North York Moors or as a stopover.
The Bed & Breakfast is just a two minute walk from the cobbled market square, with its many shops, cafes, pubs and restaurants.
The Gallery has three rooms with modern en suite facilities plus digital TV/DVD and free Wi-Fi internet access.
Delicious locally sourced breakfasts served.

18 Kirkgate, Thirsk YO7 1PQ • Tel: 01845 523767
e-mail: kathryn@gallerybedandbreakfast.co.uk
www.gallerybedandbreakfast.co.uk

Ryedale House　*Established 30 years* Exclusive to non-smokers, welcoming Yorkshire house of character at the foot of the moors, National Park "Heartbeat" country. Three-and-a-half-miles from Whitby. Magnificent scenery, moors, dales, picturesque harbours, cliffs, beaches, scenic railways, superb walking - it's all here! Highly commended, beautifully appointed rooms with private facilities, many extras. Guest lounge; breakfast room with views over Esk Valley. Enjoy the large south-facing terrace and landscaped gardens. Extensive traditional and vegetarian breakfast choice. Local inns and restaurants - two within a short walk. Parking available, also public transport

Bed and Breakfast: double £30-£32pppn, single £33pppn, minimum stay two nights • Weekly reductions all season.
Monday-Friday 4 night offers available (not high season) • Regret, no pets or children.

Mrs Pat Beale, Ryedale House, 156 Coach Road, Sleights, Near Whitby YO22 5EQ
Tel & Fax: 01947 810534 • www.ryedalehouse.co.uk

SB

York

YORK. Cumbria House, 2 Vyner Street, Haxby Road, York YO31 8HS (01904 636817).
A warm and friendly welcome awaits you at Cumbria House - an elegant, tastefully decorated Victorian guest house, where comfort and quality are assured. We are convenient for the city, being only 15 minutes' walk from York's historic Minster and yet within minutes of the northern by-pass (A1237). A launderette, bank and children's park are close by. All rooms have colour TV, radio alarms and tea/coffee facilities. Most are en suite and all are non-smoking.
Rates: Bed and Breakfast from £27 to £30 per person.
 • Full English breakfast or vegetarian alternative • Non-smoking.
 • Central heating • Fire Certificate.

SB

AA ★★★, VisitBritain ★★★.
e-mail: candj@cumbriahouse.freeserve.co.uk　　　　www.cumbriahouse.com

---

York

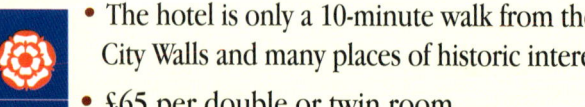

York

York

symbols

 Totally non-smoking

 Children Welcome

 Suitable for Disabled Guests

 Pets Welcome

 SB *Short Breaks available*

 Licensed

Doncaster

South Yorkshire

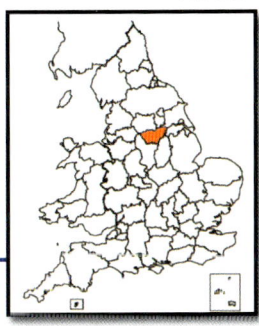

Rock Farm

**Rock Farm, Hooton Pagnell,
Doncaster DN5 7BT
Tel/Fax: 01977 642200
Mobile: 07785 916186
e-mail: info@rockfarm.info
www.rockfarm.info**

SB

A warm welcome and a hearty breakfast await guests at this Grade II Listed stone farmhouse on a 200-acre mixed farm. Situated in the picturesque stone-built village of Hooton Pagnell, six miles north-west of Doncaster, 5 minutes from the A1 and Brodsworth Hall, 10 minutes M62, M1 and M18. Open all year.

Single, double or twin rooms and a twin-bedded suite.

Family rooms from £70, Double rooms from £60
Twin from £50, Single from £28

West Yorkshire

West Yorkshire is a mix of wild moorland and towns and cities with a long industrial heritage. Spend time in one of the many fascinating museums of past working life, then stride out over the moors, taking in the dramatic scenery, before a shopping spree or a wonderful afternoon tea. Leeds is the destination for a lively city break. Theatres, ballet, opera, festivals, restaurants, clubs, and of course, one of the best shopping experiences in the country, all are here to provide entertainment and a memorable stay. Visit the exclusive shops in the Victoria Quarter and find sought after brands in the new developments at The Light and Clarence Dock on the waterside. If all this is too much for some family members, Harewood House with its wonderful interior, gardens, and adventure playground is nearby, as well as the Yorkshire Planetarium.

SB

If you are looking for a warm and comfortable environment in which to relax and enjoy your stay whilst visiting Yorkshire then The Manor will be perfect for you. This luxurious 5 Star Gold Award retreat offers a relaxing and refreshing base from which to explore some of the most beautiful countryside in Yorkshire. Lovingly restored, this 18th Century Manor House is enhanced by many original features. Ideally situated for exploring the rugged Pennine moorland or Bronte Country, the Yorkshire Dales and beyond.

- Ample off-road car parking
- Centrally heated en suite rooms
- Welcome tray with homemade biscuits
- Top quality beds and linen
- Satellite TV with DVD player
- Wi-Fi Internet access
- Extensive DVD library
- Hairdryer, CD player & radio alarm clock
- Easy access to all major attractions
- Debit & credit cards accepted
- Private guest lounge
- Thick fluffy towels
- Extensive complimentary toiletries
- Iron & ironing board available
- Packed lunches available on request
- Hearty Yorkshire breakfast menu

The Manor Guest House
Sutton Drive, Cullingworth, Bradford BD13 5BQ
Tel: 01535 274374
e-mail: info@cullingworthmanor.co.uk
www.cullingworthmanor.co.uk

Beamish

Durham

SB

If you're looking for a few days' break somewhere different, why not go to Durham? Set between the North Pennines Area of Outstanding Natural Beauty and the Durham Heritage Coast on the meandering River Wear, the old medieval heart of the city of Durham with its cobbled streets is dominated by the cathedral and castle, a World Heritage Site, and a must for visitors. On the way back to the modern shopping centre, browse through individual boutiques and galleries in the alleys and vennels, and the stalls of the Victorian market, then enjoy a stroll along the riverside walks. Don't miss the wildflower meadows or the exotic trees and tropical glasshouses at Durham University Botanic Gardens, and just outside the city visit medieval Crook Hall with its English theme gardens and maze.

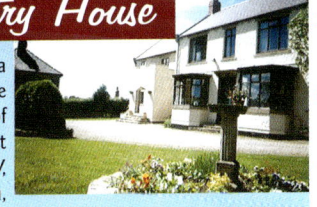
High Force, the highest waterfall in England, on the Raby Castle estate, is easily accessible. Include it in a long distance hike or a gentle wander from the car park. While in the vicinity, pay a visit to this magnificent medieval castle itself near Middleton-in-Teesdale. Hire bikes in Hamsterley Forest, where there are trails for every level of ability, or take a picnic and wander through the woodland., Life at the beginning of the 19th and 20th centuries is re-enacted at the Beamish Museum, a working town, colliery and farm. Enthusiasts will make for Head of Steam, the Darlington Railway Museum to see Locomotive No 1, driven by Stephenson himself on the opening of the very first railway line. At Killhope go underground at the lead mining museum, and try the hands-on activities. There are always fun and interesting things to do on the days when the sun isn't shining so brightly.

Northumberland

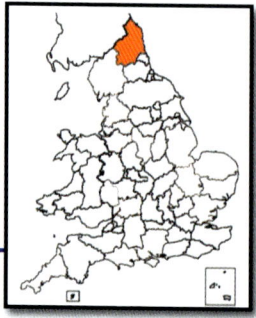

B I L T O N   B A R N S

Located between Alnwick and Alnmouth and set in beautiful countryside, Bilton Barns is a 390-acre traditional Northumberland mixed farm. The farmhouse has full central heating, a guests' lounge, dining room and a sun lounge designed to take full advantage of the magnificent views . The four spacious, antique furnished bedrooms all have en suite bathrooms. There is one king-sized four-poster, one room with king-sized sleigh bed plus a single bed, one twin /super king-sized double bedded room and one king-sized double bedded room. All have TV with Freeview, hospitality trays, clock/radio and soft fluffy towels.

Start your day with a delicious home cooked traditional farmhouse breakfast - try the famous local Craster kippers or choose from the extensive selection of fresh alternatives.

Bilton Barns B&B is close to the many places of interest that this super part of Northumberland offers, including Alnwick, Alnmouth, Warkworth, Bamburgh, Craster, Seahouses, The Farne Islands and Lindisfarne to name but a few.

Bed and Breakfast accommodation is open all year except Christmas / New Year. Sorry no pets.

Brian & Dorothy Jackson, Bilton Barns, Alnmouth, Alnwick, Northumberland, NE66 2TB
Tel : (01665) 830427 Fax: (01665) 833909 • e-mail : stay@biltonbarns.com • www.biltonbarns.com

Rambling over the heather-clad Cheviot moorlands, exploring the castles and pele towers built to ward off invading Scots, watching the feast of wildlife on the coast and in the countryside, breathing in the wonderful sea air on a golden sandy beach, you'll find it all in Northumberland. On the coast, a designated Area of Outstanding Natural Beauty, keen walkers can take the Coast Path from the walled Georgian market town of Berwick-on-Tweed to Cresswell, stopping at little fishing villages on the way. At the lively market town of Alnwick visit the castle, Hogwarts in the Harry Potter films, with the newly redeveloped gardens, magnificent water features and even a poison garden! Rare and endangered wildlife is found all along the coast and the ultimate destination for enthusiasts is the Farne Islands, with boat trips from the family resort of Seahouses to watch the grey seals and seabirds. In the heather moorlands of the Cheviot Hills there are plenty of opportunities for birdwatching, as well as horse riding, fishing, canoeing and rock climbing.

Alnwick, Berwick-Upon-Tweed

Situated one minute from Berwick-upon-Tweed's main thoroughfare, this hotel is surrounded by walls and ramparts built by Queen Elizabeth I to protect Berwick.

Accommodation consists of two family rooms, one double, one twin/triple and one single room (can sleep up to 14). All are en suite with colour TV, tea/coffee, central heating, hairdryer, trouser press and ironing facilities.

The Cobbled Yard Hotel

A wide range of attractions and activities are on offer with lots of beaches and picnic areas within easy walking distance. Ideal centre point for visits to Edinburgh and Newcastle. Private parking.

Restaurant and bar lounge. Vegetarians also catered for.

Fred and Lynda Miller, Cobbled Yard Hotel,
40 Walkergate, Berwick-upon-Tweed,
Northumberland TD15 1DJ

Tel: 01289 308 407 • Fax: 01289 330 623
e-mail: enquiries@cobbledyardhotel.com
www.cobbledyardhotel.com

The Rob Roy
Dock Road,
Tweedmouth
Berwick-upon-Tweed
TD15 2BE

The Rob Roy

SB

• *Situated close to the River Tweed and just five minutes from the centre of the historic town of Berwick-upon-Tweed.*

• *Fully licensed bar area serving real ales and a good selection of wines. Beer garden with stunning river views.*

• *Harbour Lights Restaurant offering a superb range of tempting food, with local produce used where possible.*

Hosts: Linda & Ian Woods

e-mail: therobroy@hotmail.co.uk
Tel & Fax: 01289 306428

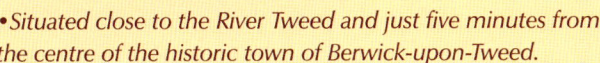

11 Quay Walls

An 18th Century Grade II Listed property in an ideal location for both city trips and walkers - Edinburgh and Newcastle between 45 minutes to one hour away.
The three en suite bedrooms, with digital TV, wireless internet and hospitality tray, have wonderful views over the river and the three famous bridges.
Full Northumbrian breakfast. No smoking.

Berwick-upon-Tweed TD15 1HB
Tel: 01289 309945
info@11quaywalls.co.uk • www.11quaywalls.co.uk

Greencarts is a working farm situated in Roman Wall country, ideally placed for exploring by car, bike or walking. It has magnificent views of the Tyne Valley. It is warm and homely, with central heating and log fires. Home-cooked food is provided. En suite accommodation with safe car/bike parking. Convenient for Hexham Racecourse; fishing available locally. All welcome. Bed and Breakfast from £25 to £40. Open all year. Campsite and bunk barn also available.

Mr & Mrs D Maughan, Greencarts Farm,
Humshaugh, Hexham NE46 4BW
Tel/Fax: 01434 681320
e-mail: sandra@greencarts.co.uk.

GREENCARTS FARM
www.greencarts.co.uk

Holmhead

Standing directly on The Hadrian's Wall Path and Pennine Way, Holmhead is built with stones from Hadrian's Wall and stands on the foundations of this World Heritage Site.
Ideal for exploring Hadrian's Wall, the Lake District, Scottish Borders and North Pennines.

All bedrooms en suite. Beautiful country views.

Self-catering cottage sleeps four. Camping Barn also available.

Holmhead Guest House
Hadrian's Wall
Greenhead
Northunberland CA8 7HY
Tel: 016977 47402
e-mail:
holmhead@forestbarn.com
www.bandbhadrianswall.com

Bush Nook Guest House
Hadrian's Wall Country

Experience the wildness, freshness, culture and two millennia of history

Bush Nook Guest House is a traditional farmhouse situated within the wonderful Hadrian's Wall countryside, with panoramic views east to Northumberland National Park and Kielder Forest.

Comfortably furnished 4 star Bed and Breakfast accommodation, all bedrooms en suite, most with open beamed ceilings.

The area has excellent walking and cycling routes, offering open countryside, peacefulness, and fresh air. Easily accessible from both east and west.

Also available: superbly equipped 4 star self-catering holiday cottage in the Hay Barn, sleeping two people, with exceptional space and atmosphere. Sofa bed for an additional two people, ideal for a group or family unit for a cost effective holiday break.

Rooms rates including breakfast from £35pppn
Special Breaks available – see website for details.
Quote FHG to receive discount

Bush Nook, Upper Denton, Gilsland CA8 7AF
Tel: 01697 747194 • info@bushnook.co.uk
www.bushnook.co.uk

symbols

 Totally non-smoking

 Children Welcome

 Suitable for Disabled Guests

 Pets Welcome

 Short Breaks available

 Licensed

SB

SB

THE OLDE SHIP INN

Main Street,
Seahouses,
Northumberland
NE68 7RD
Tel: 01665 720200
Fax: 01665 720383

A former farmhouse dating from 1745, the inn stands overlooking the harbour in the village of Seahouses.

The Olde Ship, first licensed in 1812, has been in the same family for 100 years and is now a fully residential hotel. All guest rooms, including three with four-poster beds, and executive suites with lounges and sea views, are en suite, with television, refreshment facilities and direct-dial telephone. The bars and corridors bulge at the seams with nautical memorabilia. Good home cooking features locally caught seafood, along with soups, puddings and casseroles

www.seahouses.co.uk • e-mail: theoldeship@seahouses.co.uk

This traditional country cottage is set in beautiful terraced gardens with a stream, and is only five minutes' walk from the village, castle, river walks and sandy beaches. The accommodation is comfortably furnished and includes two double rooms and one family room. All on ground floor with washbasins, shaver points, colour TV, tea/coffee making facilities and heating; en suite available. Residents' lounge. Warkworth makes an ideal base from which to explore rural Northumberland and the Borders with their unspoilt beauty and historic interest.

Children welcome, reduced rates
Non-smokers • Private parking
Colour brochure available • Open all year
Terms from £34pppn; en suite from £36pppn.

e-mail: beck-n-call@lineone.net
www.beck-n-call.co.uk
Tel: 01665 711653

Beck'N'Call
Birling West Cottage
Warkworth NE65 0XS

Tyne & Wear

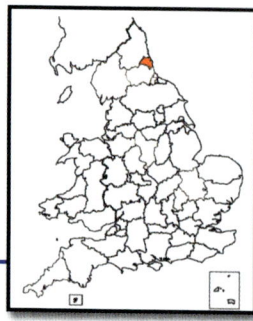

New Kent Hotel

**127 Osborne Road,
Jesmond
Newcastle-upon-Tyne
NE2 2TB**
Tel: 0191-281 7711
Fax: 0191-281 3369

SB

This privately owned
hotel is situated in a
quiet location,
but only minutes from the city centre. It has built up a reputation for
good food and friendly, efficient service in a warm and congenial
atmosphere. All bedrooms are en suite, with hospitality tray, direct-dial
telephone, colour TV with satellite, and radio. There is a spacious
cocktail lounge and a restaurant serving the best of modern and classic
cuisine. Local attractions include the MetroCentre, Northumbria
National Park, Holy Island and Bamburgh Castle.
Single from £52.50, double from £89.50.

AA
★★★

e-mail: enquiries@newkenthotel.co.uk

The FHG Directory of Website Addresses
on pages 375-392 is a useful quick reference guide for
holiday accommodation with e-mail and/or website details

Cheshire

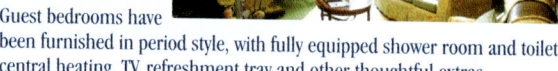

In Cheshire, just south of Manchester, combine a city break in historic Chester with a day or two at one of relaxing spas either in the city itself or in one of the luxury resorts in the rolling countryside. Time your visit to the historic Georgian mansion at Tatton Park to coincide with one of the wide choice of events held there throughout the year, including the annual RHS Flower Show. All the family will be fascinated by a visit to the giant Lovell Telescope at Jodrell Bank Visitor Centre near the old silk weaving town of Macclesfield or meeting the native animals and birdlife at the Cotebrook Shire Horse Centre. The walkways in nearby Delamere Forest provide pleasant and not too challenging walks, or hire a mountain bike to ride round the forest trails. Chester, with its wonderful array of Roman, medieval and Georgian buildings is a fascinating place to visit. Walk round the most complete example of city walls in the whole country, past the beautiful cathedral, before browsing through the wonderful range of shops, art galleries and museums.

Macclesfield, Nantwich

Northwich

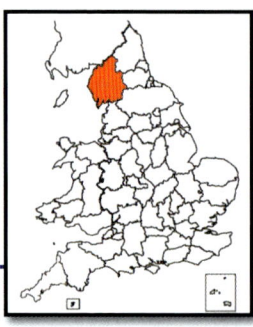
Cumbria

Alston

Ambleside

Rothay House

SB

Strictly non-smoking bed and breakfast guest house accommodation in Ambleside, near Lake Windermere

Rothay House is an attractive modern detached guest house set in pleasant gardens with views of the surrounding fells. All bedrooms are comfortable and well furnished, with en suite facilities, TV/DVD player, hairdryer, free Wi-Fi, tea and coffee trays.

Darren and Debra Hammond offer a friendly atmosphere in clean, attractive surroundings. The house is within easy walking distance of the village centre. Ambleside has a variety of interesting shops and restaurants and makes an ideal base for walking, touring or enjoying sailing, watersports and angling on Lake Windermere. Car not essential, but ample parking.

Open all year except 23-27 December.
Children over 4 years welcome; sorry, no pets.
Strictly non-smoking
B&B from £29 to £35. • Winter Breaks available.

Rothay Road, Ambleside LA22 0EE •Tel & Fax: 015394 32434
e-mail: email@rothay-house.com •www.rothay-house.com

Ambleside

Ambleside

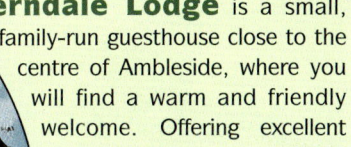

Ambleside

SB

SB

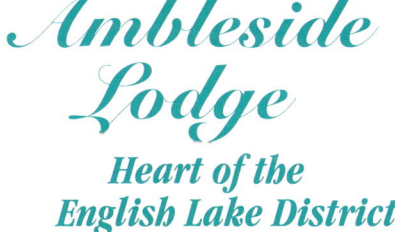

Ambleside

CROYDEN HOUSE

Church Street, Ambleside LA22 0BU
Tel: 015394 32209

Croyden House is a non-smoking guest house situated on a quiet street just a minute's walk from the main bus stop and centre of Ambleside, a popular Lakeland village offering a wide range of shops, restaurants and inns catering for all tastes. The en suite rooms have colour TV, tea/ coffee making facilities; some have views of Loughrigg and Fairfield Horseshoe.

A generous home-cooked breakfast is served and special diets catered for by arrangement. Enjoy home baked scones and cakes, light lunches and afternoon teas in our adjacent Tea Rooms. Freshly made packed lunches by arrangement - home made cake included!

Guests have the use of a private car park.

B&B from £25 - £45 pppn.
Spring and Autumn Offers
Groups Welcome

Haven Cottage

Rydal Road, Ambleside Cumbria LA22 9AY

SB

Haven Cottage offers you a comfortable, relaxed atmosphere. Conveniently situated on the edge of Ambleside with a good selection of shops, restaurants and cinemas only 3 minutes' walk away. Just a short stroll to Lake Windermere or the beautiful countryside. There are seven rooms, all en suite and including doubles, twins and family. Free wireless internet. Ample private parking. Home cooking with local produce. Cycle store and drying facilities. Visit website for photos of refurbishment.

Contact us on 015394 33270
or e-mail enquiries@amblesidehavencottage.co.uk
www.amblesidehavencottage.co.uk

Ambleside, Appleby-in-Westmorland

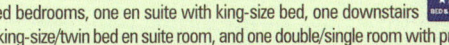

Bowness-on-Windermere, Broughton-in-Furness

SB

The region now known as Cumbria, in England's north west, has been attracting tourists since the end of the 17th century, and the number of visitors has been increasing ever since. The area is a walkers' paradise, and whether on foot, in a wheelchair or a pushchair there's a path and trail for everyone. There are magnificent views from the lakesides as well as from the hill and mountain tops, so whether you're following one of the 'Miles without Stiles' on relatively level, well laid tracks around the towns and villages, climbing in the Langdales or tackling Scafell Pike, the highest mountain in England, you won't miss out on all the Lake District has to offer. Stay in Penrith, Appleby-in-Westmorland or Kirkby Lonsdale to explore the western Pennines or Silloth-on-Solway to discover the Solway Firth coast. Finally don't miss out Carlisle and its cathedral and castle, the stronghold involved in so many battles with the Scots, the Jacobite rebellions and the Civil War.

Broughton-in-Furness, Buttermere

Cockermouth

Coniston, Elterwater (Ambleside)

symbols

  Totally non-smoking

  Children Welcome

  Suitable for Disabled Guests

 *Pets Welcome*

SB *Short Breaks available*

 *Licensed*

Kendal, Keswick

Honister House

1 Borrowdale Road, Keswick CA12 5DD
Tel: 017687 73181
John and Susie Stakes

SB

This timber-beamed house is conveniently located in Keswick town centre, in the heart of the Lake District.
The three en suite bedrooms are equipped to a high standard and Wi-Fi is available. Breakfasts use Fairtrade, organic and locally sourced produce wherever possible. Children welcome. Discounted parking permits available.

Honister House has an AA Breakfast Award and is a member of the Vegetarian Society Food and Drink Guild. Cyclists, walkers and families welcome.

email: honisterhouse@btconnect.com
www.honisterhouse.co.uk

Keswick Park House• Cumbria

SB

The Keswick Park House is family-owned and personally run with an excellent team of staff committed to helping you have a relaxed and enjoyable stay in Keswick and the Lake District. A fine Victorian house set in the heart of Keswick, close to all local shops, restaurants and pubs, but still close to the parks and mountains. All our 16 bedrooms have good quality pine or mahogany furniture, and they are also all fully en suite with bath or shower rooms. Despite being near the centre of town, many rooms boast fine views of Skiddaw, Walla Crag, or the Grizedale Range. Lounge bar/café with award-winning garden. Small private car park. We offer three-night mid-week out-of-season breaks. Please call us for details.

33 Station Road, Keswick, Cumbria, CA12 4NA
Telephone: (017687) 72072 • Fax: (017687) 74816
e-mail: info@KeswickParkHotel.com • www.KeswickParkHotel.com

SB

Bassenthwaite Hall Farm B&B

A friendly welcome awaits you at our lovely 17thC farmhouse which is fully modernised whilst retaining its olde worlde character. A charming lounge/dining room furnished with antiques is available for

guests' use any time. The delightful bedrooms have individual period furnishings and washbasins; two bathrooms nearby; annexed en suite rooms also available. Tea and coffee making facilities available. An excellent Cumbrian Breakfast starts the day, or choose a lighter option.

Single from £38 per night, Twin/Double from £30pppn, Family Room from £75 per night.

Our farmhouse is by the stream and a wooden footbridge where ducks swim happily all day. A gentle stroll further up the riverside takes you to the 17th Century village inn where good food is served.

Bassenthwaite Hall Farm, Bassenthwaite Village, Near Keswick, Cumbria CA12 4QP

Tel & Fax: 01768 776393• www.bedandbreakfast-lakedistrict.co.uk e-mail: info@loftholidaycottages.co.uk

Maple Bank Country Guest House

Rhona and Tommy extend a warm welcome to guests both old and new at Maple Bank Country Guest House, a magnificent Edwardian residence set in an acre of beautiful

gardens near the town of Keswick, right in the heart of the Lake District National Park and close to all of its many facilities.The House commands uninterrupted views across the Derwent valley towards the lofty Skiddaw and the smaller Latrigg, and is ideally placed for walking, climbing, water sports, and other less strenuous activities like fishing or visiting local pubs and eateries! We pride ourselves on the service we offer to guests and will try our utmost to make your stay as comfortable and enjoyable as possible. We have plentiful free and secure parking, secure cycle storage and a drying room

There are 5 spacious double rooms and two twin rooms, all en suite with colour TV, plentiful wardrobe space, tea & coffee making facilities, iron and ironing board (on request), and hairdryer. Our spacious yet cosy family room is en suite, with one double bed, one single bed, colour TV, plentiful wardrobe space, tea & coffee making facilities, iron and ironing board (on request), and hairdryer

★★★★
GUEST HOUSE

Maple Bank, Braithwaite, Keswick, Cumbria CA12 5RY Tel: 01768 778229 • Fax: 01768 778000 e-mail: enquiries@maplebank.co.uk • www.maplebank.co.uk

Horse & Farrier Inn
Threlkeld, Keswick CA12 4SQ

The Horse & Farrier has enjoyed an idyllic location in the centre of the picturesque village of Threlkeld, just 4 miles east of Keswick in Cumbria, for over 300 years. Built in 1688 and situated beneath Blencathra, with stunning views looking over towards the Helvellyn Range, this traditional Lakeland Inn offers a warm Cumbrian welcome to all its customers.

Mellow Lakeland stone, traditional architecture and such a peaceful setting make the Horse & Farrier a perfect place to enjoy a quiet pint, delicious food or a short break "away from it all". With superb Lakeland walks on your doorstep including Blencathra and Skiddaw and the Cumbria Way, we're ideally situated for walkers.

Our Restaurant is well known locally for the quality and imagination of its food and our Bar serves some of the best Jennings real ales in the Lake District.

Together with our well appointed en suite bed & breakfast accommodation, this really is a special place to spend some time.

Tel: 017687 79688 • Fax: 017687 79823
info@horseandfarrier.com www.horseandfarrier.com

West View
Guest House

Close to Derwent Water in Keswick and located in the heart of the beautiful English Lake District, West View Guest House offers luxury en suite bedrooms with 38 channel digital TV, clock radio, hair dryer, and tea/coffee tray (with a mountain of tea and coffee). Guests are welcome to use the large lounge all day as a refuge for rest and planning. West View overlooks Hope Park and is close to the Theatre and the boat landings for tours of Derwent Water.

View from the lounge window

Paul and Dawn Titley, The Heads,
Keswick, Cumbria CA12 5ES
Tel: 017687 73638
info@westviewkeswick.co.uk
www.westviewkeswick.co.uk

Keswick

SB

Littletown Farm

Littletown Farm, Newlands,
Keswick, Cumbria CA12 5TU
Tel: 017687 78353
e-mail: info@littletownfarm.co.uk
www.littletownfarm.co.uk

Littletown Farm is a traditional working Lakeland farm offering bed & breakfast accommodation in the beautiful, unspoilt Newlands valley, in the heart of the Lake District National Park.

In a unique location nestled at the foot of Catbells, the farm was the inspiration behind Beatrix Potter's Mrs Tiggywinkle stories. The beautiful Northern fells surround the accommodation, providing spectacular scenery and remarkable tranquillity, an ideal retreat to get away from it all.

Licensed bar, large dining room, comfortable TV lounge, wi-fi access and large enclosed garden. Each bedroom has its own stunning view looking directly onto the fells.

Traditional Farmhouse breakfast, packed lunches arranged if required.

8 rooms in total, 6 of which have private facilities, each room with tea & coffee making facilities. 2 family rooms available.

Double/twin rooms from £38pppn including Full Lakeland Breakfast.

Lindisfarne Guest House

21 Church Street, Keswick CA12 4DX
Tel: 017687 73218

A cosy, friendly guest house with home cooking and hearty breakfasts. Situated within a residential area close to the town centre of Keswick and within easy walking distance of Lake Derwentwater and Fitz Park.

We have en suite rooms, all with colour TV, tea/coffee facilities and central heating.

Bed and Breakfast from £30.00pppn.

Chris and Alison Burns look forward to welcoming you.

e-mail:alison230@btinternet.com
www.lindisfarnehouse.com

Keswick, Kirkby Lonsdale

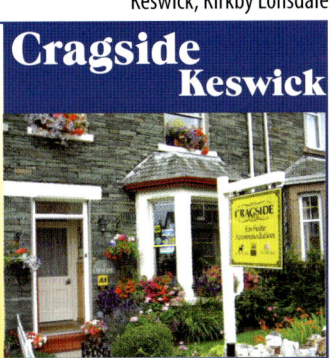

symbols

 Totally non-smoking

 Children Welcome

 Suitable for Disabled Guests

 Pets Welcome

SB *Short Breaks available*

 Licensed

Black Combe House
Kirksanton, Cumbria LA18 4NW

In a quiet village location, in SW Cumbria, Black Combe House offers hearty breakfasts and comfortable rooms with rural views. There are 5 double rooms, 1 twin room, 1 single room and 1 family room, all en suite with TV, DVD, hospitality tray, shaver plug and hair dryer. The very comfortable guests' lounge has TV, books, magazines and games and internet access is available. Non-smoking. Pets not allowed. Directly opposite Black Combe House, there is the village green and in front of the house, ample parking space. The popular tourist towns and villages of The Lake District are not far away for visits.

Ed & Dot Williams.
Tel: 01229 776683 or 07879 531290
www.blackcombehousebandb.co.uk

Riverside B&B
10 Selby Terrace, Maryport CA15 6NF
Tel: 01900 813595

Clean, welcoming Victorian townhouse, family-run. Many original features including stained glass entrance, staircase, fireplaces, coving etc. No smoking. Ideal base for the Lake District and Coastal Route. Cyclists and Walkers Welcome. Fishing available (sea and river). Delicious full English breakfast and towels provided. Colour TV and tea/coffee facilities in all rooms. Packed lunch available.

Standard rooms: one single, one double and one family (double and two single beds also used as a twin/double/triple), from £22pppn.
One double en suite room available from £25pppn.　　　　Contact: Mrs L. Renac.

Near Sawrey, Newby Bridge,

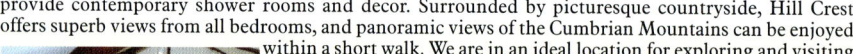

FHG Guides publish a large range of well-known accommodation guides. We will be happy to send you details or you can use the order form at the back of this book.

The FHG Directory of Website Addresses
on pages 375-392 is a useful quick reference guide for holiday accommodation with e-mail and/or website details

Windermere

New rooms, new dining experience, same fabulous location...

Nestling in a peaceful setting in the Gilpin Valley, The Wild Boar benefits from beautiful surrounding countryside, including its own private woodland for guests to enjoy, whilst exploring the rest of the National Park is easy with many other Lake District attractions close by.

New, individually designed bedrooms boast some unique features such as copper bath and log fires, as well as modern touches like iPod docking stations, flat screen TV's and DVD players providing even more creature comforts.

An exciting new Grill and Smokehouse with open kitchen and chef's table, a choice of real ales, guest beers, an extensive wine list and a range of over 50 whiskies.

Locally produced seasonal ingredients, a classic British hearty menu and an excellent ambience - which is famously The Wild Boar.

The
Wild Boar
Inn, Grill & Smokehouse
★★★★

T 08458 504 604
thewildboarinn.co.uk

English Lakes
Hotels Resorts & Venues

Windermere

Lancashire

Generations of excited holiday-makers have visited Lancashire's coastal resorts, and amongst them Blackpool stands out as the star attraction. For seaside fun, amusements and entertainment it's difficult to beat, but the quieter resorts along the coast with traditional seaside attractions have their own appeal. For an outdoor break there are all kinds of activities from hot air ballooning to fishing on offer inland, from the lowland plain, along the winding valleys of the Ribble and the Lune, up into the Forest of Bowland and on to the moors of the western Pennines. There's fun for all ages in Blackpool, Britain's most popular resort, from the Big Wheel on Central Pier, the thrilling rides at the Pleasure Beach, and the Winter Gardens with award-winning shows, jazz and rock concerts, to the tropical sharks and reef fish at Sealife, the Sandcastle Waterpark, and a ride in a historic tram along the newly renovated Central Promenade, not forgetting sand, sea and donkey rides.

Parr Hall Farm

ETC/AA ★★★★

SB

Within an hour of the Lake District, Yorkshire Dales, Peak District, Chester and North Wales, Parr Hall Farm is an ideal base for touring the local area. Attractions nearby include Camelot Theme Park, Martin Mere, Southport, Blackpool and antiques at Bygone Times, Heskin Hall, Park Hall and Botany Bay. All rooms are en suite, with central heating. Good food nearby. Ground floor rooms. Off-road parking.

From M6 take A5209 for Parbold, then immediately take B5250 right turn for Eccleston. After five miles, Parr Lane is on the right, the house is first on the left.

B&B from £35 per person, reductions for children.

Parr Hall Farm, Eccleston, Chorley PR7 5SL
01257 451917• Fax: 01257 453749
enquiries@parrhallfarm.com • www.parrhallfarm.com

SB

Rose Cottage

A warm welcome awaits in our exclusively non-smoking 200-year-old cottage. At the gateway to the Ribble Valley, an ideal stop when visiting Scotland, only 30 minutes' drive to Blackpool and the 5 miles from the M6 J31, ideal for walkers and cyclists, also business persons wanting a friendly, homely environment. Each well equipped room offers guests a comfortable, relaxing stay; all have private facilities, welcome tray, flat-screen TV with Freeview, wi-fi and fridge. Laptop available for guest use.

Off-road parking, including covered parking for motorbikes and cycle lock. Pets welcome.

e-mail: bbrose.cott@talk21.com • www.rosecottagebandb.com
Tel: 01254 813223 • Fax: 01254 813831
LONGSIGHT ROAD (A59), CLAYTON-LE-DALE, NEAR MELLOR,
RIBBLE VALLEY, LANCASHIRE BB1 9EX

SB

Rakefoot Farm
Chaigley, Near Clitheroe BB7 3LY
Tel: (Chipping) 01995 61332 or 07889 279063
Fax: 01995 61296 • e-mail: info@rakefootfarm.co.uk
website: www.rakefootfarm.co.uk

Family farm in the beautiful countryside of the Ribble Valley in the peaceful Forest of Bowland, with panoramic views. Ideally placed for touring Coast, Dales and Lakes. 9 miles M6 Junction 31a. Superb walks, golf and horse riding nearby, or visit pretty villages and factory shops. Warm welcome whether on holiday or business, refreshments on arrival.

BED AND BREAKFAST or SELF-CATERING in 17th century farmhouse and traditional stone barn conversion. Wood-burning stoves, central heating, exposed beams and stonework. Most bedrooms en suite, some ground floor. Excellent home cooked meals service, pubs/restaurants nearby. Garden and patios. Dogs by arrangement. Laundry.

B&B £25 - £35pppn sharing, £25 - £40pn single
S/C four properties (3 can be internally interlinked)
£111 - £695 per property per week. Short breaks available.

A large detached bungalow, three miles south of Lancaster and 400 yards from Lancaster University. Access from M6 Junction 33 and A6.

Two double bedrooms each with shower, toilet, colour TV and tea/coffee making facilities. One bedroom also has a private TV lounge. Full central heating. Spacious parking. A good location for visiting Blackpool, Morecambe, the Lake District and Yorkshire Dales. You will be sure of a friendly welcome and a homely atmosphere.

Bed and Breakfast from £25 per person • Sorry, no pets
Non-smokers only please • Open all year

Roy and Helen Domville, Three Gables, Chapel Lane,
Galgate, Lancaster LA2 0PN • 01524 752222

Scotland

Torran House, Drumnadrochit (page 325)

Aberdeen, Banff & Moray

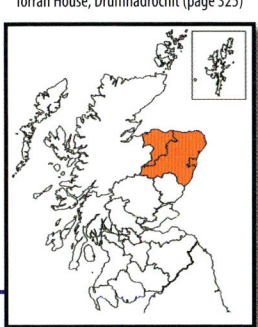

Alford, Banchory

CAMBUS O'MAY HOTEL

Ballater, Aberdeenshire AB35 5SE
Tel & Fax: 013397 55428
www.cambusomayhotel.co.uk

SB

Situated four miles east of the picturesque Deeside Village of Ballater, the Cambus O'May Hotel provides a haven of peace and tranquillity, yet affords direct access to the A93 Aberdeen to Perth road. Set in sixteen acres of attractive wooded grounds the hotel overlooks the River Dee and the hills beyond.

The Hotel, which has been owned and run by the McKechnie family for over quarter of a century, provides warm and friendly service with cuisine and comfort to match.

Originally a Victorian hunting lodge built in 1874 this Country House has been carefully modernised to provide 12 tastefully furnished bedrooms, all in keeping with the ambience of the building.

All rooms have en suite facilities, colour television, hairdryer and individually controlled heating. Hospitality trays are available on request, otherwise we would be delighted to serve early morning tea or coffee in your room.

The elegant residents' lounge with comfortable seating and open fire overlooks the front gardens and the valley beyond. It is here that guests may relax, enjoy a chat with friends, perhaps take afternoon tea or finish off their meal with coffee, mints and liqueurs.

Our unique pine-clad lounge bar with its log fire is the perfect place for a pre-dinner drink or to just unwind at the end of an eventful day.

The dining room which has panoramic views across the Dee Valley is the ideal place to enjoy the excellent cuisine offered from the table d'hôte menu which changes daily. The menu makes use of the best of local produce and can be complemented by a range of fine wines from our cellar.

The hotel welcomes families, the large grounds offering children scope to explore in safety and our close proximity to the Cambus O'May to Ballater walkway provides a traffic free environment to cycle or walk to the nearby village of Ballater.

The area makes an ideal base for enjoying the myriad of pursuits available including golfing/ fishing, shooting, cycling, hill walking and even gliding. The Whisky Trail is easily followed from Deeside and Balmoral Castle is only one of many splendid historic buildings and castles to be visited in the Grampian Region.

Scottish
TOURIST BOARD
★★★
COUNTRY HOUSE
HOTEL

SB

Reaching out into the North Sea from the Moray Firth in the north, extending south past Royal Deeside and dominated by the Grampian Highlands to the west, Aberdeenshire, Banff and Moray present a wonderful combination of countryside, coast and heritage for the holidaymaker to explore. Easily accessible from Aberdeen, where there are all the attractions of city life, this is an ideal corner of the country for an interesting and relaxing break. Why not follow one of the five tourist trails to see the spectacular scenery and learn more about the area at the same time? On the Victorian Heritage Trail follow in the footsteps of Queen Victoria to Royal Deeside to reach the best-known castle of all, Balmoral, visiting many of her favourite towns and viewpoints on the way. Golfers have 45 inland courses to choose from, some long-established, others more modern developments, like Inchmarlo, as well as the championship links.

Angus & Dundee

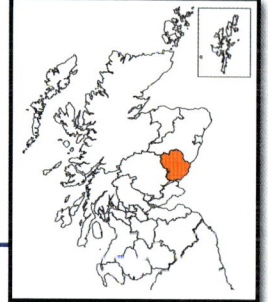

Brathinch is an 18th century farmhouse on a family-run working arable farm, with a large garden, situated off the B966 between Brechin and Edzell.

Rooms are en suite, TV and tea/coffee making facilities. Shooting, fishing, golf, castles, stately homes, wildlife, swimming and other attractions are all located nearby.

Easy access to Angus Glens and other country walks. Open all year.

Double £26pppn, twin £27pppn, single £30pppn.

We look forward to welcoming you.

Brathinch Farm
By Brechin DD9 7QZ
01356 648292 • Fax: 01356 648003
brathinch@tesco.net

SB

Muirhouses Farm

Muirhouses is a livestock and arable farm set amidst beautiful Angus countryside, close to the Cairngorm National Park.

The accommodation is very comfortable with en suite rooms and central heating.

Every comfort is assured, from the homely welcome on arrival to the delicious breakfast. An excellent base for golf, walking and cycling.

**Cortachy, Kirriemuir,
Angus DD8 4QG**
Tel: 01575 573128 • *Mrs S. McLaren*
e-mail: susan@muirhouses.plus.com
www.muirhousesfarm.co.uk

Argyll & Bute

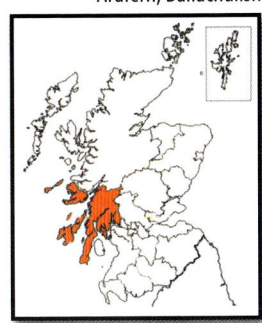

SB

The Argyll Arms Hotel, located on the waterfront of the village of Bunessan, and close to the famous
Isle of Iona, provides accommodation, bar and restaurant facilities on the beautiful Isle of Mull.

With spectacular sea and island views, the hotel is the perfect base from which to explore, either by car
or on foot if walking is your forte, or by bike. We can arrange bike hire or why not bring your own?
Secure storage is available and bikers are most welcome. The new owners invite you to enjoy their
friendly and relaxed Scottish hospitality in comfortable accommodation, value-for-money bistro-style
food and the unique atmosphere of the Isle of Mull. All rooms en suite.

Open all day 365 days of the year catering for residents and non residents.

Argyll & Bute is a wonderfully unspoilt area, historically the heartland of Scotland and home
to a wealth of fascinating wildlife. Here you may be lucky enough to catch a glimpse of an
eagle, a wildcat or an osprey, or even a fine antlered stag. On the upper reaches of Loch
Caolisport can be found St Columba's Cave, and more recent times are illustrated at the
Auchindrain Highland Township south of Inveraray, a friendly little town with plenty to see,
including the Jail, Wildlife Park and Maritime Museum. Bute is the most accessible of the
west coast islands, and Rothesay is its main town. Explore the dungeons and grand hall of
Rothesay Castle, or visit the fascinating Bute Museum. The town offers a full range of leisure
facilities, including a fine swimming pool and superb golf course.

Inveraray, Isle of Gigha

Killean Farmhouse

Killean Farmhouse is located just a few miles outside Inveraray. Ideally situated for walking, climbing, pony trekking or just touring. There is fishing for trout, pike or salmon, and opportunities to enjoy boating, water skiing or windsurfing. The whole area is steeped in history and the town of Inveraray itself is a classic example of 18th century Scottish town planning.

Bed & Breakfast accommodation is available in 5 en suite rooms in the main house, and in cottages set round a courtyard, all with a living room and small kitchen area (breakfast served in main house). Well behaved dogs welcome.

Mrs Semple, Killean Farmhouse, Inveraray PA32 8XT
Tel: 01499 302474 • www.killean-farmhouse.co.uk

SB

Gigha Hotel

The community-owned Isle of Gigha (Gaelic: God's Island) is known as The Jewel of the Inner Hebrides. The Atlantic's crystal clear waters surround this six-mile long magical isle, and lap gently on to its white sandy beaches - creating an aura of peace and tranquillity.

The Gigha Hotel caters admirably for the discerning holidaymaker with comfortable accommodation and first class cuisine, including fresh local seafood. There are also holiday cottages available.

A must for any visitor is a wander around the famous sub-tropical Achamore Gardens, where palm trees and many other exotic plants flourish in Gigha's mild climatic conditions.

The Isle of Gigha Heritage Trust retails quality island-related craft products, some of which have utilised the Trust's own tartan. Other activities on offer include organised walks, bird watching, sea fishing, a nine-hole golf course and alternative therapies.

Call us on **01583 505254** Fax: **01583 505244**
www.gigha.org.uk

symbols

  Totally non-smoking   *Pets Welcome*

  Children Welcome   **SB** *Short Breaks available*

  Suitable for Disabled Guests   *Licensed*

The Falls of Lora Hotel
Connel Ferry, By Oban PA37 1PB
Oban 5 miles, only 2½-3 hours' drive north-west of Glasgow/Edinburgh.

Overlooking Loch Etive, this fine owner-run Victorian hotel with a modern extension offers a warm welcome, good food, service and comfort. 30 bedrooms including 7 luxury rooms (one with four-poster and round bath, another with a 7' round bed and Jacuzzi bathroom), standard twins and doubles, inexpensive family rooms with bunk beds. Relax in the lochside garden across the road, or in the super Cocktail Bar with open log fire and over 100 brands of whisky to tempt you. The attractive and comfortable bistro has an extensive and varied menu. An ideal centre for touring, sailing and walking.

Tel: 01631 710483 • Fax: 01631 710694
e-mail: enquiries@fallsoflora.com • www.fallsoflora.com

Small, family-run guest house where we aim to make your stay as comfortable as possible. All rooms have central heating, colour TV and hospitality trays; some en suite. A full Scottish breakfast is served, although Continental is available if preferred. We have ample private parking at the rear of the house. Situated 10 minutes' walk from the town centre, train, boat and bus terminals. Oban boasts regular sailings to the Islands, and an excellent golf course, as well as walking, cycling, fishing, or just letting the world go by.

A warm welcome awaits you all year round.

MRS STEWART, GLENVIEW, SOROBA ROAD, OBAN PA34 4JF • Tel: 01631 562267
e-mail: morven.stewart@hotmail.co.uk

A warm welcome awaits you in this delightful bungalow set in 20 acres of farmland where we breed our own Highland cattle which graze at the front. It is a peaceful location as we are set back from the road, and an ideal spot for touring, with the main ferry terminal at Oban just 10 minutes away. Our luxurious rooms have their own special sitting room attached where you can enjoy your coffee or a glass of wine in peace, and we also have our own restaurant where you can dine.

Mrs J. Currie, Hawthorn, 5 Kell Crofts, Benderloch, Oban PA37 1QS • 01631 720452
e-mail: june@hawthorncottages.com
www.hawthorncottages.com

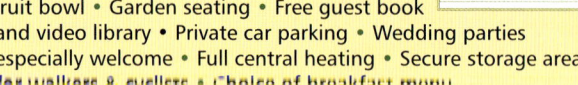

Ayr

Ayrshire & Arran

Leslie Anne
GUEST HOUSE
13 CASTLEHILL ROAD, AYR KA7 2HX

Chris and Jennifer extend a warm welcome to their comfortable Victorian guest house, situated close to Ayr town centre and railway station, with links to Prestwick Airport (5 miles) and Glasgow Airport (30 miles).

• All bedrooms are en suite • Ground floor rooms available
• Full cooked Scottish breakfast or continental breakfast • Private parking
• Internet facilities

Ideally positioned for guests to enjoy Ayr's shopping centre and wide variety of bars and restaurants. An excellent base to explore Ayrshire, South West Scotland and the Clyde Coast. Glasgow city centre is only an hour away by train. Ayrshire's famous golf courses are all near by.

Phone: 01292 265646
e-mail: leslieanne2@btinternet.com
www.leslieanne.org.uk

SB

Ayrshire and The Isle of Arran is situated in the South of Scotland, flanked by the Borders to the south and the Central Belt to the north. Here the warm waters of the Gulf Stream meet with miles of sandy beaches and a dramatic coastline littered with rocky outcrops and caves, once a favourite with smugglers. The Island of Arran, as well as being one of Scotland's most accessible islands, is also arguably one of its most truly representative. From the mountainous north, including Goat Fell, highest peak in the south of Scotland, to the undulating south it is easy to see how the island became known as "Scotland in miniature". The Burns National Heritage Park near Ayr celebrates the life and works of Scotland's national poet. Visitors may enjoy a visit to Ayr Racecourse, enjoy a shopping spree, or a round on one the area's 44 golf courses.

Ayr

SB

Sunnyside

BED AND BREAKFAST
26 Dunure Road, Alloway, Ayr KA7 4HR

4-Star accommodation close to Burns Cottage, Alloway, birthplace of Robert Burns. We are praised for our **superb service**, **spacious, well furnished double, twin or family bedrooms** and **excellent breakfasts** using **local produce**.
Just 5 minutes' walk from the beach and the River Doon.
Good bar restaurant 5 minutes' walk, or we can provide home-made soup and sandwiches. Whatever your requirements, we will be pleased to cater for them. *Mrs Helen R Malcolm*

helen@ayrbandb.co.uk
www.ayrbandb.co.uk
Tel: 01292 441234 • Mobile 07801 556 594

Langley Bank Guest House

39 Carrick Road, Ayr KA7 2RD • 01292 264246

A well appointed Victorian house offering high standards of acccommodation at affordable prices. Centrally located and within walking distance of the town centre, local attractions and golf courses. Double/twin en suite rooms and an en suite family room.

4* luxury accommodation • See website for visual tour

Also available for self-catering - a brand new 3 bedroom penthouse apartment offering spectacular views over Arran. Ideal for golfing parties. Secure underground parking.

e-mail: enquiries@langleybank.co.uk • www.langleybank.co.uk

Comfortable friendly accommodation is offered on this 200 acre dairy farm well situated for the A736 Glasgow to Irvine road and for the A737; well placed to visit golf courses, country parks, or leisure centre, also ideal for the ferry to Arran or Millport and for many good shopping centres all around.

A high standard of cleanliness is assured by Mrs Gillan who is a first class cook holding many awards, food being served in the diningroom with its beautiful picture windows.

Three comfortable bedrooms (double en suite, family and twin), all with tea-making facilities, central heating and electric blankets. Two bathrooms with shower; sittingroom with colour TV. Children welcome.

Bed and Breakfast from £18 double room; en suite from £23. Dinner can be arranged.

**Mrs Jane Gillan, Shotts Farm, Beith KA15 1LB
Tel & Fax: 01505 502273 • e-mail: shotts.farm@btinternet.com**

SB

symbols

 Totally non-smoking

 Children Welcome

 Suitable for Disabled Guests

 Pets Welcome

SB *Short Breaks available*

 *Licensed*

Brodick

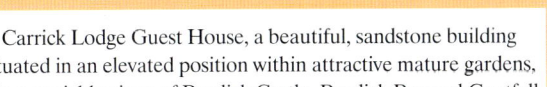

Carrick Lodge

SB

Carrick Lodge Guest House, a beautiful, sandstone building situated in an elevated position within attractive mature gardens, enjoys enviable views of Brodick Castle, Brodick Bay and Goatfell.

A relaxed and friendly guest house with spacious accommodation, large dining room and residents' lounge offering panoramic views of the Arran hills.

We provide a warm, friendly welcome to all our guests and can cater for speciality diets in our dining room.

All bedrooms are en suite and come complete with full amenities including television, ironing facilities, hair dryers and tea and coffee making facilities. Free wi-fi internet access. Off-road parking if travelling by car, but Brodick is only a 10 minute walk if on foot.

Arran has something to offer everyone. It is a delight for hillwalkers and climbers and with 7 golf courses, golfers too. Horse riding and trekking are available from two centres on the island and for more of a challenge there is paragliding and quad biking.

Double, twin and single rooms from £32pppn.

Carrick Lodge, Brodick, Isle of Arran KA27 8BH
Tel: 01770 302 550 • Mobile: 07766 074762 • www.carricklodge.co.uk

---

Open all year
Terms from £22pppn

SB

SUNNYSIDE – a very special place to stay with its south easterly unrestricted rural and coastal views across the bonny Clyde on the beautiful Isle of Arran. Enjoy this view over a scrumptious full breakfast; relax in the comfort and cleanliness of the double en suite, or twin bedded room (with private bathroom) both having shower over bath. Located in Kings Cross, 8 miles south of Brodick; and convenient for good restaurants/pubs.

Mrs Evelyn Coles, "Sunnyside",
King's Cross, Isle of Arran KA27 8RG
Tel: 01770 700422 or 0771 800 5688

South Whittlieburn Farmhouse B&B
and Caravan & Camping,
Brisbane Glen, Largs KA30 8SN
Tel: 01475 675881 • Fax: 01475 675080

Superb farmhouse accommodation with lovely scenic views on our working sheep farm in peaceful Brisbane Glen. Ample parking. Only five minutes' drive from the popular tourist resort of Largs and near the ferries to the islands. 40 minutes from Glasgow and Prestwick airports. Warm friendly hospitality, enormous delicious breakfasts. All rooms en suite.

Chosen by "WHICH? TOP TEN BEST BED & BREAKFAST", WELCOME HOST.
Nominated for AA LANDLADY OF THE YEAR 2005/06 • Bed & Breakfast from £30pppn.

Caravan and camping site on our farm 2½ miles north east of Largs; electric hook-ups, toilet and shower, from £13 per night. Caravan for hire. Also self-catering flat available at Dunoon. Open all year except Christmas.

A warm welcome from Mary Watson. Enjoy a great holiday at South Whittlieburn Farm,
for a holiday you will want to repeat where guests become friends.

e-mail: largsbandb@southwhittlieburnfarm.freeserve.co.uk
www.ukcampsite.co.uk
www.SmoothHound.co.uk/hotels/whittlie.html

A warm welcome awaits you at our family farm situated in the beautiful Doon Valley. An ideal base for touring Ayrshire or Galloway on the Galloway Tourist Route (A713), 6 miles south of Ayr.

Our spacious farmhouse offers en suite twin/double and family rooms with king size beds and all facilities, lounge, dining room and large garden. We serve a delicious varied farmhouse breakfast, with homebaking and farm produce in season. Enjoy a bedtime tea/coffee or hot chocolate with a home baked cookie. Prestwick Airport guests welcome (whatever the time!). Children and pets welcome. B&B from £22.50 pppn, children half price.

Smithston Farm, Patna, By Ayr KA6 7EZ
Mrs Joyce Bothwell - 01292 531211
e-mail: bothwellfarming@onetel.com
www.smithstonfarmhouse.co.uk

Prestwick

Readers are requested to mention this FHG guide
when seeking accommodation

Other British holiday guides from **FHG Guides**

PUBS & INNS · 300 GREAT HOTELS
SHORT BREAK HOLIDAYS
The bestselling and original PETS WELCOME!
THE GOLF GUIDE - Where to Play, Where to Stay
SELF-CATERING HOLIDAYS · 500 GREAT PLACES TO STAY
CARAVAN & CAMPING HOLIDAYS · FAMILY BREAKS

Published annually: available in all good bookshops or direct from the publisher:
FHG Guides, Abbey Mill Business Centre, Seedhill, Paisley PA1 1TJ
Tel: 0141 887 0428 • Fax: 0141 889 7204
e-mail: admin@fhguides.co.uk • www.holidayguides.com

Borders

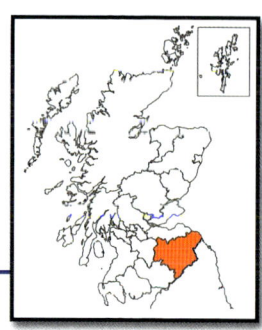

SB

Judy Cavers, CROSSHALL FARM,
Greenlaw, Duns, Berwickshire TD10 6UL

A warm welcome awaits you at Crosshall Farm, just off the A697. The house is furnished in traditional style. The bedrooms are decorated to a high standard with a beautiful guest room overlooking the Cheviot Hills. We are in an ideal situation for touring the lovely Border countryside where there is plenty to see, historic market towns, castles, stately homes, walks and lots of golf courses. We are also about 30 minutes from the coast. Bed and Breakfast from £30 per person for twin room with private bathroom and double room en suite. Both rooms have tea/coffee making facilities and TV. After a long and tiring day it's nice to relax in the lounge with a cup of tea and home-made baking.

tel: 01890 840220 • mobile: 07812 801399
e-mail: judycavers@aol.com • www.crosshallfarm.co.uk

Traditional Georgian house, set well away from the road in its own spacious grounds • Peaceful and relaxing atmosphere • Good touring base • A warm welcome awaits you, in a comfortable country house with lovely views • Accommodation consists of one single room and two twin rooms • Lift to local pub for supper to accommodate walkers • Quiet peaceful location with ample parking space • Terms from: £40 single, £30pp in twin room.

Mainhill

Contact: Mrs Lee, Mainhill House, St Boswells, Melrose, Roxburghshire TD6 0HG0
Tel: 01835 823788
e-mail: annmainhill@hotmail.co.uk

Fauhope Country House

a secluded country house with views that have inspired artists, writers, poets and musicians over the centuries.

Fauhope, in the heart of the Scottish Borders, has been renovated with great style and attention to detail and offers luxurious Bed and Breakfast accommodation in three guest bedrooms, all of which are spacious and en suite. There is a beautiful drawing room for reading, chatting and relaxing, and extensive grounds and gardens. A generous Full Scottish Breakfast is served in the dining room, or choose something lighter if you prefer. The house is ideally located for visiting places of interest throughout the Borders region and Edinburgh City Centre is only a 60-minute drive away.

Fauhope, Gattonside, Melrose, Roxburghshire TD6 9LU • Tel: 01896 823184 • info@fauhopehouse.com • www.fauhopehouse.com

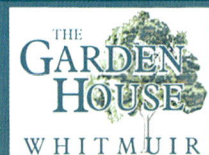

 is a modern four-bedroom detached house located in a quiet situation near the centre of the conservation village of West Linton, which is on the A702, the main Edinburgh to Carlisle road, with handy access to Edinburgh and central Scotland.

All bedrooms have tea/coffee making facilities, TV and hairdryer.

Full range of quality breakfasts available including traditional English or scrambled egg with smoked salmon and oatcakes. Evening meals available by prior arrangement. Pets welcome. Parking.

Terms from £25pppn twin, £30pppn single,
£30pppn double/twin en suite.

Mrs M. Thain, The Meadows Bed and Breakfast,
4 Robinsland Drive, West Linton EH46 7JD
01968 661790 • e-mail: mwthain@btinternet.com
www.themeadowsbandb.co.uk

Covering about eighteen hundred miles, The Scottish Borders stretch from the rolling hills and moorland in the west, through gentler valleys to the rich agricultural plains of the east, and the rocky Berwickshire coastline with its secluded coves and picturesque fishing villages. Through the centre, tracing a silvery course from the hills to the sea, runs the River Tweed which provides some of the best fishing in Scotland. As well as fishing there is golf – 18 courses in all, riding or cycling and some of the best modern sports centres and swimming pools in the country. Friendly towns and charming villages are there to be discovered, while castles, abbeys, stately homes and museums illustrate the exciting and often bloody history of the area. It's this history which is commemorated in the Common Ridings and other local festivals, creating a colourful pageant much enjoyed by visitors and native Borderers alike.

Castle Douglas

Dumfries & Galloway

Castle Douglas, Gatehouse of Fleet, Gretna Green

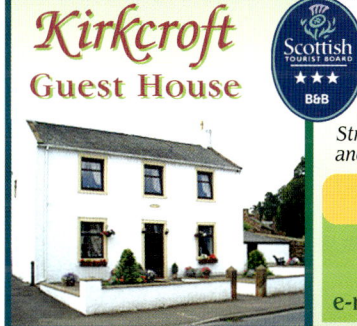

Dumfries & Galloway is a mixture of high moorland and sheltered glens, and presents abundant opportunities for hill walking, rambling, fishing for salmon and sea trout, cycling, bird watching and field sports. There are at least 32 golf courses, ranging from the challenging Stranraer course at Creachmore to the scenic, clifftop course at Portpatrick. The Stranraer course has the distinction of being the last course designed by James Braid. The warming influence of the Gulf Stream ensures a mild climate which makes touring a pleasure, and many visitors come here to visit the dozens of interesting castles, gardens, museums and historic sites. In addition, pony trekking and riding plus a never-ending succession of ceilidhs, village fairs, country dances, classical music concerts and children's entertainment guarantee plenty of scope for enjoyment.

Edinburgh & Lothians

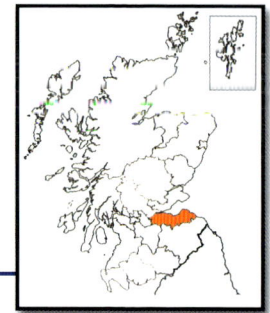

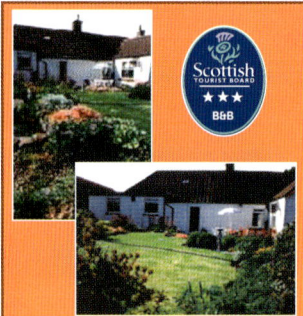

SB

This 17th century farmhouse is situated two miles from M8 Junction 4, which is midway between Glasgow and Edinburgh. This peaceful location overlooks panoramic views of the countryside. All rooms are on the ground floor, ideal for disabled visitors, and have central heating, colour TV and tea/coffee making facilities. We are within easy reach of golf, fishing, cycling (15 mile cycle track runs along back of property). Ample security parking. Open January to December. Pets and children by arrangement.

Twin Room from £45-£55, Family Room from £60-£80.

Mrs F. Gibb, Tarrareoch Farm, Station Road, Armadale, Near Bathgate EH48 3BJ • 01501 730404
e-mail: nicola@gibb0209.fsnet.co.uk

SB

Ardgarth Guest House · *Portobello* · *Edinburgh*

A warm and comfortable family-run Guest House, tastefully adapted to suit couples, friends, family groups and single travellers. Rooms are either en suite or standard (with wash basins). The rooms are of generous size, clean, warm and comfortably furnished. Two rooms on the ground floor are fully accessible to disabled guests.
• Free wifi and free internet access available in guest lounge.
• Cots, high chairs and baby listening can be arranged.
1 St Mary's Place, Portobello, Edinburgh EH15 2QF
Tel: 0131 669 3021
www.ardgarth.com • stay@ardgarth.com

SB

INTERNATIONAL GUEST HOUSE • EDINBURGH

Conveniently situated 1½ miles south of Princes Street on the main A701, on the main bus route. Private parking. All bedrooms en suite, with direct-dial telephone, colour TV and tea/coffee making facilities. Some rooms enjoy magnificent views across to the extinct volcano of Arthur's Seat. The full Scottish breakfasts served on the finest bone china are a delight. Contact Mrs Niven for details. B&B from £35 to £75 single; £60 to £130 double.

37 Mayfield Gardens, Edinburgh EH9 2BX
Tel: 0131 667 2511 • Fax: 0131 667 1112
e-mail: intergh1@yahoo.co.uk • www.accommodation-edinburgh.com

AA ★★★★ Guest House

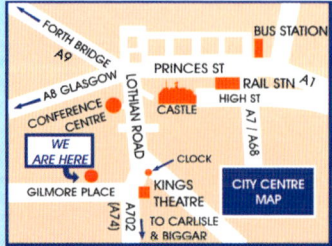

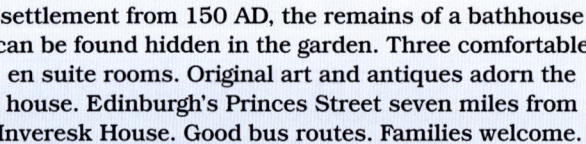

In the area known as Edinburgh & The Lothians, Scotland's capital is home to a wide range of attractions offering something for visitors of all ages. The Royal Mile holds many of the most historic sights, but within a short distance there are fine gardens to visit or the chance to sample the latest in interactive technology. A network of signposted paths allow walkers of all abilities to enjoy the contrasts of the area, whether for a leisurely stroll or at a more energetic pace. The annual Festival in August is part of the city's tradition and visitors flock to enjoy the performing arts, theatre, ballet, cinema and music, and of course "The Tattoo" itself. At the Festival Fringe there are free shows and impromptu acts, a jazz festival and book festivals. East Lothian has beautiful countryside and dramatic coastline, all only a short distance from Edinburgh. Once thriving fishing villages, North Berwick and Dunbar now cater for visitors who delight in their traditional seaside charm.

symbols

 Totally non-smoking

 Children Welcome

 Suitable for Disabled Guests

 Pets Welcome

SB *Short Breaks available*

 Licensed

Anstruther

Fife

SB

Fife - whether as 'County', 'Region' or more traditionally 'Kingdom', this has always been a prosperous part of Scotland. The coast, with small ports such as Crail, Anstruther, Pittenweem, St Monance, Elie and the more commercial Methil, Burntisland and Kirkcaldy, has always been interesting and important. St Andrews with its university, castle, cathedral and golf, is the best known and most visited town. Dunfermline has a historic past with many royal associations and was the birthplace of the philanthropist, Andrew Carnegie.Cupar, Falkland, Kinross (for Loch Leven), Auchtermuchty and Leuchars are amongst the many other historic sites in Fife, and at North Queensferry is one of Fife's most popular attractions, Deep Sea World.

Glasgow & District

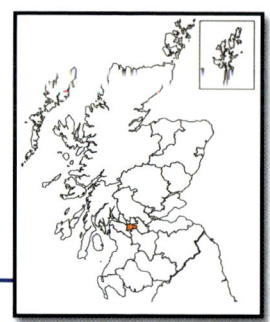

symbols

 Totally non-smoking

 Children Welcome

 Suitable for Disabled Guests

 Pets Welcome

 SB Short Breaks available

 Licensed

Allanfauld Farm

Allanfauld Bed and Breakfast is open all year round. Enjoy a warm Scottish welcome and true farmhouse hospitality at our family home, where we have farmed for almost 100 years. The working farm sits at the foot of the Kilsyth Hills, a great base to explore central Scotland.

Twin/triple/family room • Single room
Both rooms have TV and tea/coffee making facilities. Visitors have access to a TV and lounge room and WI-FI connection.

Both Glasgow and Stirling are a 20 minute drive away. Croy Train Station is two miles away, where a short train journey will take you into the centre of Glasgow, Edinburgh or Stirling.

There is local access to a wide range of activities and facilities such as a swimming pool, a rock-climbing hotspot, golf courses, hill-walking, fishing and many other tourist attractions, such as Stirling Castle, The Colzium Estate and The Antonine Wall. The starting point for The West Highland Way is located in Milngavie, only a 30 minute drive away.

B&B from £25-£30.

www.allanfauld.com

The Lodge
available as self-catering or with breakfast served in farmhouse. Sleeps 2/4.

Libby MacGregor, Allanfauld Farm, Kilsyth, Glasgow G65 9DF
Tel & Fax: 01236 822155
e-mail: allanfauld@hotmail.com

Log cabins now available

Highlands

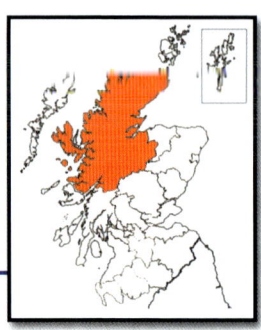

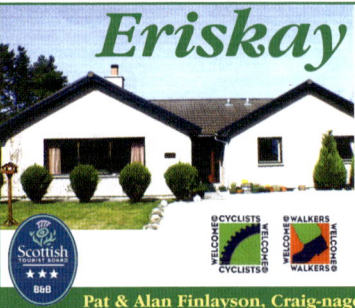

GLENURQUHART

House

HOTEL

Peaceful Tranquillity

Drumnadrochit - Loch Ness - Glen Affric

Escape to the Scottish Highlands

for peace and tranquillity and stay in our comfortable and friendly STB 4 Star Restaurant with Rooms. With fantastic views of Loch Meikle and Glen Urquhart, the house nestles in six acres of wooded grounds close to Loch Ness and Glen Affric nature reserve.

All bedrooms are en suite and have tea/coffee making facilities, hairdryer, colour TV/DVD and bathrobes.

There is a cosy lounge bar warmed by a log fire and an award-winning restaurant serving freshly cooked meals.

We are ideally situated for exploring the Highlands of Scotland; day trips might include visits to the Isle of Skye, a trip to the Highland capital of Inverness or a boat trip to spot dolphins on the Moray Firth.

View of Loch Meikle from the Hotel

GLENURQUHART HOUSE HOTEL

Balnain, Drumnadrochit IV63 6TJ

Carol and Ewan Macleod • Tel: 01456 476234

info@glenurquhart-house-hotel.co.uk • www.glenurquhart-house-hotel.co.uk

Apart from the stunning scenery, the major attraction of The Scottish Highlands is that there is so much to see and do, whatever the season. Stretching from Fort William in the south, to Wick in the far north, there is a wealth of visitor attractions and facilities. Loch Ness, home of the legendary monster, is perhaps the most famous of these attractions and the Loch Ness Visitor Centre also provides a variety of souvenirs, including kilts and whisky. The Clansman Centre, The Rare Breeds Park and The Caledonian Canal Heritage Centre are also worth a visit. Fort William in the Western Highlands is a busy town with a wide range of shops and services, pubs, restaurants and Scottish entertainment. The West Highland Museum in the town illustrates the tale of Bonnie Prince Charlie and the Jacobites.

• We are a family-run guest house situated in the Highland village of Ballachulish. Set on the shores of Loch Leven and only one mile from the

majesty of Glencoe, Ballachulish makes an ideal centre for exploring much of Scotland's natural beauty. Attractions in and around Glencoe, Fort William, Oban, Skye, Mull, Loch Ness, Loch Lomond and many others are easily accessible.

Imposing craggy mountains, beautiful lochs, waterfalls and forestry can all be found locally and wildlife such as seals, dolphins, otters, deer, pine-martens and eagles thrive. There are a multitude of beautiful and interesting walks, from strolls to view historic Glencoe or around the Lochan trails to mainland Britain's most challenging mountain ridge - Glencoe's Aonach Eagach (The Notched Ridge).

• All of our rooms have en suite facilities, colour TV, DVD player, hospitality tray and individually controlled room heaters.

• We have a comfortable guest lounge, snack bar, separate dining room, drying room, bike store and large car park.

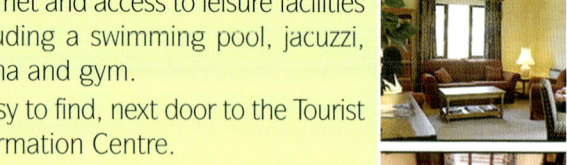

• We can also offer our guests wi-fi internet and access to leisure facilities including a swimming pool, jacuzzi, sauna and gym.

• Easy to find, next door to the Tourist Information Centre.

• B&B from £20.

Mike and Christine Richardson
Strathassynt Guest House, Loanfern,
Ballachulish, Near Glencoe PH49 4JB
Tel: 01855 811261
e-mail: info@strathassynt.com
www.strathassynt.com

Grantown-on-Spey, Invergarry

The North West Highlands is home to the nation's first Geopark, underlining the importance of the area's geological past. The famous Inverewe Gardens with its wonderful array of foreign plants, more formal borders and lovely views everywhere is worth a visit at any season. John O'Groats is, of course, the ultimate destination of most travellers as it was for the Norsemen centuries ago, whose heritage is preserved in the Northlands Viking Centre at Auckengill. The main towns in this sparsely populated area are Dornoch, Golspie, Brora and Helmsdale. Opportunities exist throughout the Highlands for all kinds of water sports, and the Caledonian Canal is ideal for cruising holidays, or yachting. Other activities include walking, cycling, pony trekking and golf, and anglers will find good sea fishing, as well as some great value day permits for fresh water fishing.

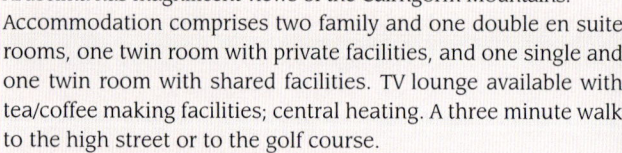

symbols

 Totally non-smoking   *Pets Welcome*

 Children Welcome   **SB** *Short Breaks available*

 Suitable for Disabled Guests   *Licensed*

A warm welcome awaits guests at this family-run guesthouse. All the spacious rooms are en suite, with central heating and hospitality tray, and enjoy lovely views over mountain and forest. Two of the ground floor rooms are suitable for disabled visitors. Situated about ten miles north of Kyle of Lochalsh, we offer traditional Scottish hospitality.

Margaret & Gerry Arscott
SOLUIS MU THUATH GUEST HOUSE
Braeintra, by Achmore, Lochalsh IV53 8UP
Tel: 01599 577219

Whether you are touring, biking, walking or just soaking up the atmosphere, Soluis Mu Thuath is in the ideal location for exploring some of the most dramatic scenery in the Western Highlands

Visit Skye, Plockton, Torridon, Applecross and Glenelg or enjoy some of the many challenging (and less challenging) walks.

B&B from £28 • Non-smoking

e-mail: soluismuthuath@btopenworld.com
www.highlandsaccommodation.co.uk

SB

Poolewe • Wester Ross

SB

Bruach Ard overlooks beautiful Loch Ewe at Inverasdale near Poolewe in Wester Ross. We are an informal, family-run B&B (non-smoking), comprising two double bedrooms and one twin bedroom (all en suite), comfortable guest sitting room with TV (Sky connected), video, board games, CD player, local guidebooks, maps and brochures. The sitting room and guest dining room overlook the Loch. Full cooked and/or continental breakfast. Fresh local produce is used where possible. Packed lunches and evening meals by arrangement. Pets welcome. STB ★★★ B&B.

e-mail: dgeorge@globalnet.co.uk
Tel: 01445 781765 • www.davidgeorge.co.uk

SB

The Old Inn at Reay in Caithness is truly a piece of Scottish history. It was originally built in 1739 as an Inn serving both travellers and the people of the village of Reay. The original building is still intact and in use as a private home and a bed and breakfast establishment today. Jean and Derek Murray are your hosts at The Old Inn and their objective is to make your stay a very special one. To this end, they have developed bedrooms to keep you comfortable, and both a breakfast and evening meal to make you feel very special indeed. Ideal base for touring the far north of Scotland, or catching the ferry to Orkney.

The Old Inn
Reay, Thurso KW14 7RE

derek.theoldinn@btinternet.com
www.theoldinnatreay.co.uk
Tel: 01847 811554

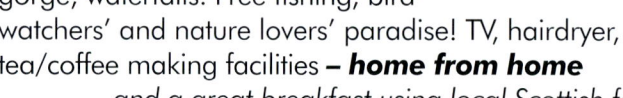

This former 19th century coaching inn on the John O'Groats peninsula is set in six acres of parkland, close to the Queen Mother's former Highland home, the Castle of Mey.

Fully modernised, the hotel has eight centrally heated en suite bedrooms with colour television and tea making facilities; the spacious Pentland Suite offers a double and family room with en suite bathroom.

Locally caught salmon, crab and other fine Highland produce feature on the varied table d'hôte and grill menus available in the Garden Room, while lighter meals and snacks can be enjoyed in the cosy Pentland Lounge.

A warm Highland welcome awaits you.

www.castlearms.co.uk
Tel & Fax: 01847 851244
e-mail: castlearms.mey@btinternet.com

THE CASTLE ARMS HOTEL
Mey, By Thurso,
Caithness KW14 8XH

WHITEBRIDGE HOTEL

Proprietors David & Sarah welcome you to Whitebridge Hotel, where an atmosphere of comfort and quiet goes hand in hand with traditional character. The hotel has stunning views of the Monadhliath Mountains. 12 en suite bedrooms, all with colour TV and tea/coffee making. • Excellent home-prepared food served in the cosy dining room. Comfortable residents' lounge. • Two bars.

Excellent brown trout fishing in the area.

Whitebridge, Loch Ness South
IV2 6UN • 01456 486226

AA ★★ HOTEL

e-mail: info@whitebridgehotel.co.uk • www.whitebridgehotel.co.uk

The FHG Directory of Website Addresses

on pages 375-392 is a useful quick reference guide for
holiday accommodation with e-mail and/or website details

Readers are requested to mention this FHG guide
when seeking accommodation

Lanarkshire

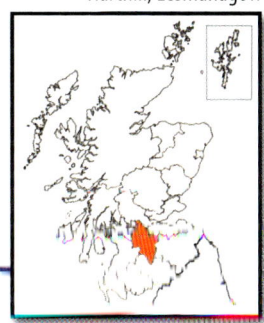

Perth & Kinross

One double, one double four-poster and one double/twin on ground floor. All rooms en suite with tea/coffee making facilities, radio and TV; ironing and hair drying facilities. Comfortable lounge with colour TV; diningroom. Heating throughout. Vegetarian meals; home cooking and baking; full cooked breakfast. Places of interest range from Scott's 'Discovery' in Dundee to Edinburgh Castle. Also golf, fishing and walking. Pets by arrangement.

B&B from £28.50 to £30pp, discounts for Senior Citizens.

**Rosalind Young, Holmrigg, Wester
Essendy, Blairgowrie PH10 6RD
Tel & Fax: 01250 884309
e-mail: info@holmrigg.co.uk
www.holmrigg-bnb.co.uk**

Set just outside the village of Crianlarich, Inverardran House is sited in an elevated position with views across Strathfillan to Ben Challum.
This property offers excellent fishing, walking and touring prospects.
We can offer you Bed and Breakfast accommodation for up to nine people in two double rooms and one twin (all en suite) and one triple room with a private bathroom.
Tea/coffee making facilities in the rooms. Self-catering also available.
*Open all year • Prices from £23 to £26 per person per night based on two sharing,
£8 surcharge for a single person. Discounts for longer stays
Evening meals and packed lunches on request.*

**John and Janice Christie, Inverardran House, Crianlarich FK20 8QS
Tel: 01838 300240 • e-mail: janice@inverardran.demon.co.uk
www.inverardran.demon.co.uk**

Glenearn House,
Perth Road, Crieff
PH7 3EQ
Tel: 01764 650111

Yann's

at Glenearn House is a busy restaurant with rooms in Crieff, the gateway to the Highlands. The ambience is relaxed while the bistro has a real convivial atmosphere.

The emphasis is on good food, kept simple and traditional, and featuring many bistro classics and a few Savoyard specialities.

We have six spacious bedrooms, all with en suite shower room or adjoining bathroom, and a large lounge where you can relax.

info@yannsatglenearnhouse.com
www.yannsatglenearnhouse.com

Merlindale

is a luxurious Georgian house situated close to the town centre. All bedrooms are en suite, two with sunken bathrooms. Jacuzzi, garden, satellite television and off-road parking all available. There is a large library available for you to browse in.

Merlindale is Michelin rated, multi AA Red Diamond, and multi Glenturret Tourism Award winner.
A sumptuous family home waits to welcome you.

Merlindale, Perth Road, Crieff PH7 3EQ

Enquiries: please call
01764 655205 or
e-mail: merlin.dale@virgin.net
www.merlindale.co.uk

Perth & Kinross embraces both Highland and Lowland. Close to where the two Scotlands meet, a cluster of little resort towns has grown up: Crieff, Comrie, Dunkeld, Aberfeldy, and Pitlochry, set, some say, right in the very centre of Scotland. Perthshire touring is a special delight, as north-south hill roads drop into long loch-filled glens - Loch Rannoch, Loch Tay or Loch Earn, for example. No matter where you base yourself, from Kinross by Loch Leven to the south to Blairgowrie by the berryfields on the edge of Strathmore, you can be sure to find a string of interesting places to visit. If your tastes run to nature wild, rather than tamed in gardens, then Perthshire offers not only the delights of Caledonian pinewoods by Rannoch and the alpine flowers of the Lawers range, but also wildlife spectacle such as nesting ospreys at Loch of the Lowes by Dunkeld. There are viewing facilities by way of hides and telescopes by the lochside. Water is an important element in the Perthshire landscape, and it also plays a part in the activities choice. Angling and sailing are two of the 'mainstream' activities on offer, or enjoy a round of golf on any of Perthshire's 40 courses, including those at Gleneagles by Auchterarder. The main town of Perth has plenty of shops with High Street names as well as specialist outlets selling everything from Scottish crafts to local pearls. With attractions including an excellent repertory theatre and a great choice of eating places, this is an ideal base to explore the true heartland of Scotland.

Callander

Stirling & The Trossachs

At the heart of Scotland, Stirling & The Trossachs has played a central role in most aspects of the nation's life. History and geography have converged here in road and rail routes, in decisive sieges and battles, in important industrial developments and heritage. The county enjoys the natural riches of the Forth valley and the economic wealth of Grangemouth and Falkirk. The town of Stirling itself is a natural tourist centre, both for its own attractions, such as the historic castle and the excellent shopping facilities, and as a base for other visitor attractions close at hand. Villages and small towns such as Drymen, Killearn, Fintry and Kippen offer hospitality and interesting outings. Loch Lomond and The Trossachs National Park is less than an hour from Glasgow, yet feels worlds apart from the bustle of city life. Explore wild glens and sparkling lochs, and for the more energetic, low-level walking, cycling, and hill walking can be enjoyed.

Strathyre

Scottish Islands

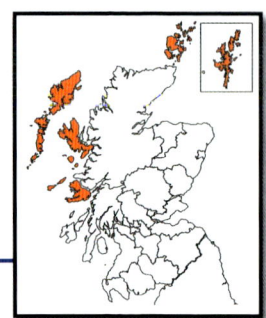

Leverburgh

Carminish House
Bed and Breakfast

Secluded, spacious, traditionally built B&B, with three twin/double en suite rooms, lounge with panoramic views over the Sound of Harris.

Payphone, satellite TV, Wi-Fi.

Ideal place to explore the Western Isles. Garden and parking.

Full Scottish breakfast.

Excellent local places to eat.

Non-smoking. Children and pets welcome.

Contact Howard and Sallie Lomas, 1A Strond, Leverburgh, Isle of Harris HS5 3UD

Tel: 01859 520400

e-mail: info@carminish.com www.carminish.com

symbols

 Totally non-smoking   *Pets Welcome*

 Children Welcome   *Short Breaks available*

 Suitable for Disabled Guests   *Licensed*

Hillview is a large house with stunning views over Broadford Bay towards Torridon and Applecross.
The B&B has a double bedroom with en suite facilities, a double bedroom with shared facilities, and a twin room with shared facilities, as well as a family room with a private bathroom and a balcony. We offer a full Scottish breakfast or vegetarian option if you prefer. Our rooms are very comfortable and most have stunning sea views.

Hillview B&B is an ideal base for exploring surrounding area. The scenery is wild and dramatic, with the Cuillin range being the island's most famous feature. The landscape varies from the strange rock formations of the Quirang to the lushness of the Garden of Skye in the south of the island. Around Broadford there are numerous mountain and coastal walks for all abilities.

Isabel MacLeod, Hillview, Blackpark, Broadford, Isle of Skye IV49 9DE
e-mail: isabel@hillview-skye.co.uk • Telephone: 01471 822 083
www.hillview-skye.co.uk

Kirkwall, Rousay

The FHG Directory of Website Addresses
on pages 375-392 is a useful quick reference guide for
holiday accommodation with e-mail and/or website details

Please note...

Anglesey

Bangor University (page 350)

Anglesey & Gwynedd

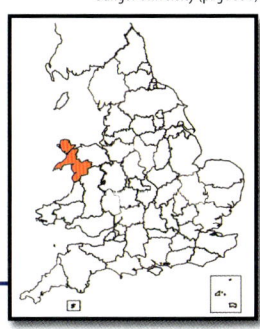

Time, space and freedom to explore beautiful
NORTH WALES

Minutes from the stunning mountains of Snowdonia and the glorious beaches of Anglesey, North Wales offers an experience unlike any other. Historical landscapes, mythical legends, arts and crafts as well as a taste of the modern; the space to explore them all is in abundance.

Let the dramatic scenery inspire you while our facilities at Bangor University impress you. With a dedicated team of staff on hand throughout your stay, we have everything you need to ensure your time with us is memorable.

So whether you're a group of 3 or a company of 300, if you're looking for an inspirational location, nature's own adventure playground, or a place to rest your head between activities in North Wales, then join us at Bangor.

We offer :

Catered Individual & Group Accommodation

Conference & Banqueting

Fine Dining

Corporate meeting space

Social Functions

Christmas Parties

Executive Boardroom Hire

Individually tailored packages

On site Leisure Facilities

Tel: 01248 388088   conferences@bangor.ac.uk

www.bangor.ac.uk/conferences

Criccieth

SB

Seaspray is a large, non-smoking Victorian terrace house, situated on the sea front, on the west side of Criccieth Castle on the Lleyn Peninsula. Some rooms are en suite, others have private facilities. Sea views across Cardigan Bay. Criccieth is only a short distance away from the Snowdonia National Park, which boasts some of the most beautiful and spectacular scenery in the country. Ample facilities are available for golfers, sailors, fishermen and ramblers. Cyclists and walkers welcome.

Open 10 months of the year • B&B from £30pppn.

Mrs Parker, Seaspray, 4 Marine Terrace, Criccieth LL52 0EF • Tel: 01766 522373

manya.parker@btinternet.com
www.seasprayguesthouse.co.uk

Anglesey & Gwynedd is rich in archaeological and historical heritage, and is home to a diversity of
wildlife which inhabit the cliffs, estuaries, heaths and rich farmland. Tourists love the unspoilt
beaches and extensive sands, and the popular seafront at Benllech offers miles of clean golden
sands, safe bathing, boating, fishing and windsurfing activities, as well as the usual ice cream
kiosks, seaside shops, and food. Snowdonia to the west attracts climbers and walkers, but the
less active will enjoy the 9 mile return journey on Bala Lake Railway which runs alongside Llyn
Tegid, or Bala Lake as it also known, and through the beautiful Snowdonia National Park to the
market town of Bala. The small, peaceful seaside village of Aberdovey within Snowdonia National
Park is a popular resort with a thriving little harbour and very popular with those who enjoy a
more active holiday. All kinds of watersports, including sailing, sailboarding, fishing, and boat
trips, are available, and there is also an 18-hole championship golf course.

Dulas Bay, Harlech

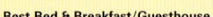

Harlech, Llannerch-y-Medd

Trearddur Bay, Tywyn

The Llyn Peninsula also boasts some of the best sailing and surfing beaches in North Wales and
its capital, Pwllheli, has an impressive marina which berths over 400 boats and has space for
overnight mooring. No holiday in the area can be complete without a visit to the Royal town of
Caernarfon with its wonderful views across the Menai Straits, and the mountains of Snowdonia
in the background. The majestic Caernarfon Castle, one of Europe's greatest medieval fortresses
famous for the investiture of Prince Charles as Prince of Wales in 1969, houses the Royal Welsh
Fusiliers Regimental Museum.

North Wales

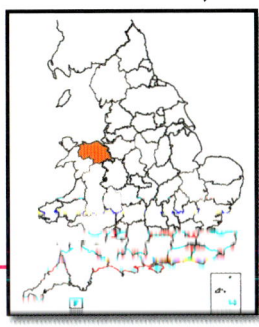

In North Wales there are charming towns and villages to explore, soft sandy beaches and rugged coastline, and as many castles, stately homes, gardens, parks, craft centres, museums and steam trains as anyone could desire. Better book a long holiday to start the grand tour, and then come back again to catch up with all that you will surely have missed. Betws-y-Coed, North Wales' most popular inland resort, houses The Snowdonia National Visitor Centre with its craft units and thrilling video presentations – always worth a visit. For fun filled family holidays try Llandudno, where a whole host of summer events and activities can be enjoyed, or Rhyl with its Children's Village on the Promenade, plus amusements, boating ponds and fairground. Walkers and cyclists will revel in the breathtaking scenery of the Prestatyn hillside and the Clwydian Range and will find all the information that they need at Offa's Dyke Visitor Centre.

Carmarthen, Llanelli

Carmarthenshire

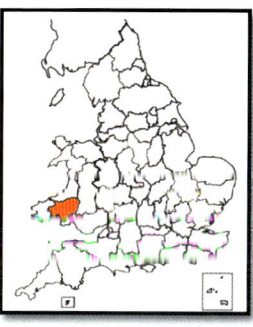

Haverfordwest

Pembrokeshire

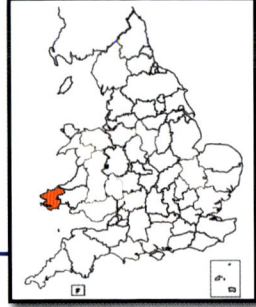

SB

Pembrokeshire's entire coastline is a designated National Park, with its sheltered coves and wooded estuaries, fine sandy beaches and some of the most dramatic cliffs in Britain. The islands of Skomer, Stokholm and Grasholm are home to thousands of seabirds, and Ramsey Island, as well as being an RSPB Reserve boasts the second largest grey seal colony in Britain. Pembrokeshire's mild climate and the many delightful towns and villages, family attractions and outdoor facilities such as surfing, water skiing, diving, pony trekking and fishing make this a favourite holiday destination.

A useful index of towns/counties appears at the back of this book

Ivybridge

Welcome to Ivybridge

Situated in a quiet part of Goodwick, Ivybridge is a friendly, family-run guest house offering comfortable accommodation just outside of Fishguard, a picturesque area of Pembrokeshire, within easy reach of the Pembrokeshire coastal paths, the historic City of St David's and beautiful beaches.

Try our small heated indoor swimming pool, relax in our conservatory or put your feet up in front of a roaring fire in the bar/lounge area and enjoy the company and atmosphere at Ivybridge.

All rooms are en suite, with Freeview television, hairdryers and hot drink facilities. Wake up to a Full Welsh Breakfast or a Continental Breakfast. Vegetarian guests are welcome and all dietary needs can be catered for. At Ivybridge we offer home cooked evening meals by arrangement using fresh locally sourced ingredients wherever possible (please book before arrival). We serve evening meals between 6.30-7.30 pm. Our guests are more than welcome to bring friends and family to dine with them. We also cater for smaller functions and parties.

For further information
please contact us

**Ivybridge, Drim Mill, Dyffryn,
Goodwick SA64 0JT
Tel: 01348 875366 • Fax: 01348 872338
e-mail: ivybridge5366@aol.com
www.ivybridgeleisure.co.uk**

Wales Cymru
★★★

Lamphey, Newport

Saundersfoot

LANGDON FARM GUEST HOUSE
Saundersfoot & Tenby

SB

Beautifully appointed, idyllic farm guesthouse on working farm overlooking two small lakes in a perfect location close to Saundersfoot and Tenby. All bedrooms en suite with central heating, colour TV, radio alarm clock and tea/coffee/hot chocolate making facilities. Separate guest sitting room with colour TV. Conservatory/breakfast room overlooking pretty gardens

and rolling countryside where horses and sheep leisurely graze while you enjoy your delicious breakfast.

Local fresh farm produce used when available. Vegetarians catered for. Perfect base for walking and touring the beautiful beaches, countryside and attractions of Pembrokeshire. Many excellent eating establishments within a short distance, from local Welsh Inns to specialist fish restaurants. Ample parking. No children under 4 years. Open January 15th - November 15th.

Bed and Breakfast £30 - £34pppn (based on two sharing). Welcome Host Gold Award.

KILGETTY, NEAR SAUNDERSFOOT SA68 0NJ • TEL: 01834 814803
e-mail: mail@stayinpembrokeshire.co.uk   www.stayinpembrokeshire.co.uk

Powys

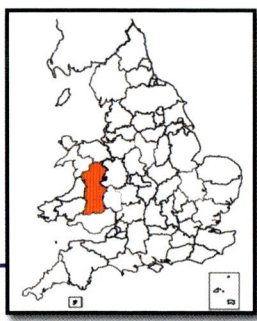

Llanbrynean is a fine, traditional, Victorian farmhouse peacefully situated on the edge of the picturesque village of Llanfrynach, 3 miles south-east of Brecon. We are in an ideal spot for exploring the area - the Brecon Beacons rise behind the farm and the Brecon/ Monmouth canal flows through the fields below.

We are a working family sheep farm with wonderful pastoral views and a large garden. The house is spacious and comfortable with a friendly, relaxed atmosphere. We have two double en suite bedrooms and one twin with private bathroom. All have tea/coffee facilities. There is a sitting room with TV. Excellent pub food within easy walking distance.

Llanbrynean

Bed and Breakfast from £28pp

Mrs A. Harpur, Llanbrynean Farm, Llanfrynach, Brecon LD3 7BQ

Tel: 01874 665222
e-mail: simon.harpur@tiscali.co.uk

Powys is situated right on England's doorstep and boasts some of most spectacular scenery in Europe. It is ideal for an action-packed holiday with fishing, golf, pony trekking, sailing and canal cruising readily available, and walkers have a choice of everything from riverside trails to mountain hikes. Offa's Dyke Path runs for 177 miles through Border country, often following the ancient earthworks, while Glyndwr's Way takes in some of the finest landscape features in Wales on its journey from Knighton to Machynlleth and back to the borders at Welshpool. There are border towns with Georgian architecture and half-timbered black and white houses to visit, or wander round the wonderful shops in the book town of Hay, famous for its Literary Festival each May. There are Victorian spa towns too, with even the smallest of places holding festivals and events throughout the year.

Newtown

SB

The Forest
COUNTRY HOUSE B&B

Hidden in the beautiful Vale of Kerry,
The Forest offers 5-star luxury bed and breakfast in
five charming en suite rooms (one with four-poster).
All bedrooms have flat screen satellite TV, DVD
player, telephone and tea tray; free Wi-Fi internet
available in all rooms. Guests can relax in the
spacious drawing room and dining room, and enjoy
the four acres of gardens, tennis court, and games
room. Kennels and stables are available.
This secluded and peaceful location is perfect to
explore the many attractions of Mid-Wales.
Self catering cottages available.

**Paul & Michelle Martin, The Forest, Gilfach Lane,
Kerry, Newtown, Powys SY16 4DW
Tel: 01686 621 821
e-mail: info@theforestkerry.co.uk
www.bedandbreakfastnewtown.co.uk**

SB

A warm welcome awaits you at Greenfields
All rooms are tastefully decorated and are spacious in size, each
having panoramic views of the rolling Kerry hills. There is a good
choice of breakfast menu and packed lunches are also available.
Accommodation available in twin, double, family and single rooms,
all en suite (twin rooms let as singles if required). Hostess tray and
TV in all rooms. The dining room has individual tables. A good place
for stopping for one night, a short break or longer holiday. Excellent
off-road parking. Brochure available.
B&B from £52 double or twin room, from £26 single and £75 family room.

**Mrs Vi Madeley, Greenfields, Kerry, Newtown SY16 4LH
Tel: 01686 670596 • Mobile: 07971 075687 • Fax: 01686 670354
e-mail: info@greenfields-bb.co.uk • www.greenfields-bb.co.uk**

Built in 1878 and once a Victorian workhouse, Brynafon Country House Hotel is now a
beautiful, comfortable, friendly, family run hotel. Set against the dramatic backdrop
of Gwastedyn Hill and the Druid's Circle and is a stone's throw from the River Wye
and the beautiful and still yet undiscovered Elan Valley.

The hotel has currently 18 individually styled, standard, deluxe and family en suite bedrooms,
some being pet friendly, 4 conference rooms, bar and restaurant.

We can cater for groups, weddings, family re-unions, and are licensed for civil ceremonies.

The Workhouse bar and restaurant serves great Welsh food all day with a good
à la carte evening menu, using local and organic produce

BRYNAFON COUNTRY HOUSE HOTEL
South Street, Rhayader, Powys LD6 5BL
Tel: 01597 810735 **Fax:** 01597 810111 **Email:** info@brynafon.co.uk
Website: www.brynafon.co.uk

Please note...

All the information in this book is given in good faith in the belief that it is correct.
However, the publishers cannot guarantee the facts given in these pages, neither are they
responsible for changes in policy, ownership or terms that may take place after the date of going to
press. Readers should always satisfy themselves that the facilities they require
are available and that the terms, if quoted, still apply.

South Wales

Monmouth (Monmouthshire)

As well as being an ideal holiday destination in its own right Swansea Bay is a perfect base for touring the rest of South Wales. A great place for all sorts of watersports such as sailing canoeing, fishing and waterskiing, or you may prefer such land based activities as walking, cycling and horse riding. Just a short journey from the City you will find the beautiful Glamorgan Heritage Coast, overlooked by dramatic cliffs. Especially popular with walkers and hikers this area is also ideal for long, leisurely strolls in the secluded coves and inlets along the coast. There are more than 15 golf courses here including the famous Royal Porthcawl. For something different visit the Wye Valley and the Vale of Usk with awesome castles, breathtaking scenery and a rich and colourful history.

SB

Tallizmand
Guest House

Llanmadoc, Gower, Swansea SA3 1DE
Tel: 01792 386373

Tastefully furnished en suite rooms. Near to beautiful secluded beaches, lined by pine forests and salt marshes. Coastal and inland walks, flowers, birds. Open all year.

B&B from £33.50 sharing a double room

- 3 double rooms (all en suite and recently refurbished to a high standard)
- ground floor rooms available
- no smoking
- special diets catered for
- tea, coffee and TV facilities in each room
- ample parking
- available 12 months a year
- large comfortable guest lounge with real fire

e-mail: tallizmandbb@aol.com
www.tallizmand.co.uk

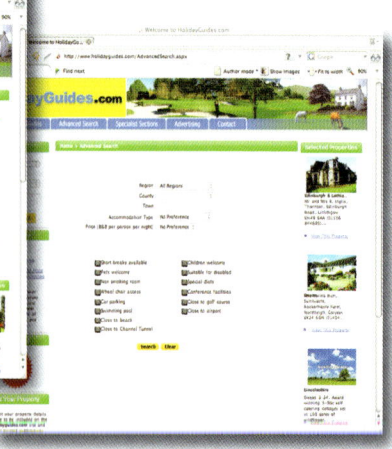

DIRECTORY OF WEBSITE AND E-MAIL ADDRESSES

A quick-reference guide to holiday accommodation with an e-mail address and/or website, conveniently arranged by country and county, with full contact details.

•LONDON

Hotel
Athena Hotel, 110-114 Sussex Gardens,
Hyde Park, LONDON W2 1UA
Tel: 020 7706 3866
• e-mail: athena@stavrouhotels.co.uk
• website: www.stavrouhotels.co.uk

Hotel
Gower Hotel, 129 Sussex Gardens,
Hyde Park, LONDON W2 2RX
Tel: 020 7262 2262
• e-mail: gower@stavrouhotels.co.uk
• website: www.stavrouhotels.co.uk

B & B
Hanwell B & B, 110a Grove Avenue,
Hanwell, LONDON W7 3ES
Tel: 020 8567 5015
• e-mail: tassanimation@aol.com
• website: www.ealing-hanwell-bed-and-breakfast.co.uk/new/index

Hotel
Queens Hotel, 33 Anson Road,
Tufnell Park, LONDON N7 0ND
Tel: 020 7607 4725
• e-mail: queens@stavrouhotels.co.uk
• website: www.stavrouhotels.co.uk

B & B
The Way to Stay, 67 Rannoch Road,
Hammersmith, LONDON W6 9SS
Tel: 020 7385 4904
• website: www.thewaytostay.co.uk

•BERKSHIRE

Touring Campsite
Wellington Country Park, Odiham Road,
Riseley, Near READING, Berkshire
RG7 1SP
Tel : 0118 932 6444
• e-mail: info@wellington-country-park.co.uk
• website: www.wellington-country-park.co.uk

Guest House
Clarence Hotel, 9 Clarence Road, WINDSOR
Berkshire SL4 5AE
Tel: 01753 864436
• e-mail: clarence.hotel@btconnect.com
• website: www.clarence-hotel.co.uk

•CHESHIRE

Farmhouse B & B
Astle Farm East, Chelford,
MACCLESFIELD, Cheshire SK10 4TA
• e-mail: gill.farmhouse@virgin.net
• website: www.astlefarmeast.co.uk

•CORNWALL

Self-catering
Penrose Burden Holiday Cottages,
St Breward, BODMIN,
Cornwall PL30 4LZ
Tel : 01208 850277
• website: www.penroseburden.co.uk

Self-Catering
Mineshop Holiday Cottages, CRACKINGTON
HAVEN, Bude, Cornwall EX23 0NR
Tel: 01840 230338
• e-mail: info@mineshop.co.uk
• website: www.mineshop.co.uk

FHG Guides

Self-Catering
Mr P. Watson, Creekside Holiday Houses, Restronguet, FALMOUTH, Cornwall TR11 5ST
Tel: 01326 372722
• website: www.creeksideholidayhouses.co.uk

Self-Catering
Mrs Terry, "Shasta", Carwinion Road, Mawnan Smith, FALMOUTH, Cornwall TR11 5JD
Tel: 01326 250775
• e-mail: katerry@btopenworld.com

Self-catering
Fowey Harbour Cottages c/o WJB Hill & Son, 3 Fore Street, FOWEY, Cornwall PL23 1AH
Tel: 01726 832211
• e-mail: hillandson@talk21.com
• website:
www.foweyharbourcottages.co.uk

Self-catering
Sandbank Holidays, St Ives Bay, HAYLE, Cornwall TR27 5BL
Tel: 01736 752594
• e-mail: info@sandbank-holidays.co.uk
• website: www.sandbank-holidays.co.uk

Self-catering
Franchis Holiday Park, Cury Cross Lanes, HELSTON, Cornwall TR12 7A2
Tel: 01326 240301
• e-mail: enquiries@franchis.co.uk
• website: www.franchis.co.uk

Caravan/Camping Park
Little Trevothan Caravan Park, Coverack, HELSTON, Cornwall TR12 6SD
Tel: 01326 280260
• e-mail: sales@littletrevothan.co.uk
• website: www.littletrevothan.co.uk

Self-catering
Mudgeon Vean Farm Holiday Cottages, HELSTON, Cornwall TR12 6DB
Tel: 01326 231341
• e-mail : mudgeonvean@aol.com
• website: www.mudgeonveam.co.uk

Self-Catering / Caravan
Mrs A. E. Moore, Hollyvagg Farm, Lewannick, LAUNCESTON, Cornwall PL15 7QH
Tel: 01566 782309
• website: www.hollyvaggfarm.co.uk

Self-catering
Butterdon Mill Holiday Homes, Merrymeet, LISKEARD, Cornwall PL14 3LS
Tel: 01579 342636
• e-mail: butterdonmillst@btconnect.com
• website: www.bmhh.co.uk

Self-Catering
Celia Hutchinson, Caradon Country Cottages, East Taphouse, LISKEARD, Cornwall PL14 4NH
Tel: 01579 320355
• e-mail: celia@caradoncottages.co.uk
• website: www.caradoncottages.co.uk

Self- Catering
Mr Lowman, Cutkive Wood Holiday Lodges, St Ive, LISKEARD, Cornwall PL14 3ND
Tel: 01579 362216
• e-mail: holidays@cutkivewood.co.uk
• website: www.cutkivewood.co.uk

Self-catering
Mr & Mrs J.Spreckley, Tremaine Green Country Cottages, Pelynt, Near LOOE, Cornwall PL13 2LT
Tel : 01503 22033
• e-mail : stay@tremainegreen.co.uk
• website : www.tremainegreen.co.uk

Self-Catering
Valleybrook Holidays, Peakswater, Lansallos, LOOE, Cornwall PL13 2QE
Tel: 01503 220493
• website: www.valleybrookholidays.com

Guest House
Mrs Dewolfreys, Dewolf Guest House, 100 Henver Road, NEWQUAY, Cornwall TR7 3BL
Tel: 01637 874746
• e-mail: holidays@dewolfguesthouse.com
• website: www.dewolfguesthouse.com

Caravan / Camping
Quarryfield Caravan & Camping Park, Crantock, NEWQUAY, Cornwall
Contact: Mrs A Winn, Tretherras, Newquay, Cornwall TR7 2RE
Tel: 01637 872792
• e-mail:
quarryfield@crantockcaravans.orangehome.co.uk
• website: www.quarryfield.co.uk

Touring Caravans / Tents
Treloy Touring Park, NEWQUAY, Cornwall TR8 4JN
Tel: 01637 872063
• e-mail: treloy.tp@btconnect.com
• website: www.treloy.co.uk

Caravan / Camping

Globe Vale Holiday Park, Radnor, REDRUTH, Cornwall TR16 4BH
Tel: 01209 891183
- **e-mail: info@globevale.co.uk**
- **website: www.globevale.co.uk**

Guest House

Mr S Hope, Dalswinton House,
ST MAWGAN-IN-PYDAR, Cornwall TR8 4EZ
Tel: 01637 860375
- **e-mail: dalswintonhouse@tiscali.co.uk**
- **website: www.dalswinton.com**

Self-Catering

Mrs R. Reeves, Maymear Cottage,
ST TUDY, Cornwall PL30 3NE
Tel: 01840 213120
- **e-mail: ruth.reeves@hotmail.co.uk**
- **website: www.maymear.co.uk**

Self-Catering

Whitsand Bay Self Catering, Portwrinkle,
TORPOINT, Cornwall PL11 3BU
Tel: 01579 345688
- **e-mail: ehwbsc@hotmail.com**
- **website: www.whitsandbayselfcatering.co.uk**

Self-Catering

The Garden House, Port Isaac, Near WADEBRIDGE, Cornwall
Contact: Mr D Oldham, Trevella, Treveighan, St Teath, Cornwall PL30 3JN
Tel: 01208 850529
- **e-mail: david.trevella@btconnect.com**
- **website: www.trevellacornwall.co.uk**

Self-Catering

Great Bodieve Farm Barns, Molesworth House, WADEBRIDGE, Cornwall PL27 7JE
Tel: 01208 814016
- **e-mail: enquiries@great-bodieve.co.uk**
- **website: www.great-bodieve.co.uk**

•CUMBRIA

Self-catering

Lakeland Hideaways, The Square, Hawkshead, Cumbria LA22 0NZ
Tel: 015394 42435
- **e-mail: bookings@lakeland-hideaways.co.uk**
- **website: www.lakeland-hideaways.co.uk**

Self- Catering

Kirkstone Foot Apartments Ltd, Kirkstone Pass Road, AMBLESIDE, Cumbria LA22 9EH
Tel: 015394 32232
- **e-mail: enquiries@kirkstonefoot.co.uk**
- **website: www.kirkstonefoot.co.uk**

Guest House / Self- Catering

Cuckoo's Nest & Smallwood House, Compston Road, AMBLESIDE, Cumbria LA22 9DJ
Tel: 015394 32330
- **e-mail: enq@cottagesambleside.co.uk**
  enq@smallwoodhotel.co.uk
- **website: www.cottagesambleside.co.uk**
  www.smallwoodhotel.co.uk

Hotel / Guest House

Mrs Liana Moore, The Old Vicarage, Vicarage Road, AMBLESIDE, Cumbria LA22 9DH
Tel: 015394 33364
- **e-mail: info@oldvicarageambleside.co.uk**
- **website: www.oldvicarageambleside.co.uk**

Hotel

Rothay Manor, AMBLESIDE, Cumbria LA22 0EH
Tel: 015394 33605
- **e-mail: hotel@rothaymanor.co.uk**
- **website: www.rothaymanor.co.uk**

Self-catering

Bowness Lakeland Holidays,
BOWNESS-ON-WINDERMERE, Cumbria
Contact: 131 Radcliffe New Road, Whitefield, Manchester M45 7RP
Tel: 0161 796 3896
- **e-mail: info@bownesslakelandholidays.co.uk**
- **website: www.bownesslakelandholidays.co.uk**

Self-catering

Ash Gill Cottages, Torver, Near CONISTON, Cumbria
Contact : Mrs D.Cowburn, "Lyndene", Pope Lane, Whitestake, Near Preston, LANCS PR4 4JR
Tel: 01772 612832
- **e-mail: dorothy@ashgillcottages.co.uk**
- **website: www.ashgillcottages.co.uk**

Self-Catering

Fisherground Farm Holidays, ESKDALE
Contact: Ian & Jennifer Hall, Orchard House, Applethwaite, Keswick, Cumbria CA12 4PN
Tel: 017687 73175
- **e-mail: holidays@fisherground.co.uk**
- **website: www.fisherground.co.uk**

Hotel

The Borrowdale Gates Hotel, GRANGE-IN-BORROWDALE, Keswick, Cumbria CA12 5UQ
Tel: 017687 77204
- **e-mail: hotel@borrowdale-gates.com**
- **website: www.borrowdale-gates.com**

Self-Catering
Mrs Almond, Irton House Farm, Isel, Near KESWICK, Cumbria CA13 9ST
Tel: 017687 76380
• e-mail: **joan@irtonhousefarm.co.uk**
• website: **www.irtonhousefarm.com**

Self-Catering
2 Moot Hall, Ireby, Near KESWICK, Cumbria CA7 1DU
Contact: Ruth Boyes, Anglers Lodge, Main Street, Helperby, North Yorkshire YO61 2NT
Tel: 01423 360759
• e-mail: **ruthboyes@virgin.net**
• website: **irebymoothall.co.uk**

Self-Catering
Mrs Trafford, Brook House Cottage Holidays, Near KESWICK CA12 4QP
Tel: 017687 76393
• e-mail: **stay@amtrafford.co.uk**
• website:
www.holidaycottageslakedistrict.co.uk

Self-Catering
Mr D Burton, Lakeland Cottage Holidays, Bassenthwaite, KESWICK CA12 4QX
Tel: 017687 76065
• e-mail: **info@lakelandcottages.co.uk**
• website: **www.lakelandcottages.co.uk**

Self-Catering
Mr D Williamson, Derwent Water Marina, Portinscale, KESWICK, Cumbria CA12 5RF
Tel: 017687 72912
• e-mail: **info@derwentwatermarina.co.uk**
• website: **www.derwentwatermarina.co.uk**

Inn
Horse and Farrier Inn, Threlkeld, KESWICK, Cumbria CA12 4SQ
Tel: 017687 79688
• e-mail: **info@horseandfarrier.com**
• website: **www.horseandfarrier.com**

Self-Catering
Mrs S.J. Bottom, Crossfield Cottages, KIRKOSWALD, Penrith, Cumbria CA10 1EU
Tel: 01768 898711
• e-mail: **info@crossfieldcottages.co.uk**
• website: **www.crossfieldcottages.co.uk**

Guest House
Beckfoot Country House, Helton, PENRITH, Cumbria CA10 2QB
Tel: 01931 713241
• e-mail: **info@beckfoot.co.uk**
• website: **www.beckfoot.co.uk**

B & B
Greenah Crag, Troutbeck, PENRITH, Cumbria CA11 0SQ
Tel: 017684 83233
• e-mail: **greenahcrag@lineone.net**
• website: **www.greenahcrag.co.uk**

Caravan Park
Tanglewood Caravan Park, Causeway Head, SILLOTH-ON-SOLWAY, Cumbria CA7 4PE
Tel:016973 31253
• e-mail:
tanglewoodcarvanpark@hotmail.com
• website:
www.tanglewoodcaravanpark.co.uk

Holiday Park
Seacote Park, ST BEES, Cumbria CA27 0ET
Tel:01946 822777
• e-mail: **reception@seacote.com**
• website: **www.seacote.com**

B & B / Self-Catering
Barbara Murphy, Land Ends Country Lodge, Watermillock, Near ULLSWATER, Cumbria CA11 0NB
Tel: 01768 486438
• e-mail: **infolandends@btinternet.com**
• website: **www.landends.co.uk**

Hotel
The Wild Boar, Crook, Near WINDERMERE, Cumbria LA23 3NF
Tel: Reservations 08458 504604
• website: **www.elh.co.uk**

•DERBYSHIRE

Self-Catering Holiday Cottages
Mark Redfern, Paddock House Farm Holiday Cottages, Peak District National Park, Alstonefield, ASHBOURNE, Derbyshire DE6 2FT
Tel: 01335 310282 / 07977 569618
• e-mail: **info@paddockhousefarm.co.uk**
• website: **www.paddockhousefarm.co.uk**

Hotel
Biggin Hall, Biggin-by-Hartington, BUXTON, Derbyshire SK17 0DH
Tel: 01298 84451
• e-mail: **enquiries@bigginhall.co.uk**
• website: **www.bigginhall.co.uk**

Caravan
Golden Valley Caravan Park, Coach Road,
RIPLEY, Derbyshire DE55 4ES
Tel: 01773 513881
• **e-mail:**
enquiries@goldenvalleycaravanpark.co.uk
• **website: www.goldenvalleycaravanpark.co.uk**

•DEVON

Self-Catering
Marsdens Cottage Holidays, 2 The Square,
Braunton, WOOLACOMBE, Devon
EX33 2JB
Tel: 01271 813777
• **e-mail: holidays@marsdens.co.uk**
• **website: www.marsdens.co.uk**

Self-Catering
Farm & Cottage Holidays, DEVON
Tel: 01237 459897
• **website: www.holidaycottages.co.uk**

Self-Catering
Wooder Manor, Widecombe-in-the-Moor,
ASHBURTON, Devon TQ13 7TR
Tel: 01364 621391
• **e-mail: angela@woodermanor.com**
• **website: www.woodermanor.com**

Hotel
Fairwater Head Hotel, Hawkchurch, Near
AXMINSTER, Devon EX13 5TX Tel: 01297
678349
• **e-mail: info@fairwaterheadhotel.co.uk**
• **website: www.fairwaterheadhotel.co.uk**

Farm B & B
Mrs J Ley, West Barton, Alverdiscott, Near
BARNSTABLE, Devon EX31 3PT
Tel: 01271 858230
• **e-mail: ela@andrews78.freeserve.co.uk**

Self-catering / B&B
Lake House Cottages and B&B, Lake
Villa, BRADWORTH, Devon EX22 75Q
Tel : 01409 241962
• **email: lesley@lakevilla.co.uk**
• **website: www.lakevilla.co.uk**

Guest House
Woodlands Guest House, Parkham Road,
BRIXHAM, South Devon TQ5 9BU
Tel: 01803 852040
• **e-mail: woodlandsbrixham@btinternet.com**
• **website: www.woodlandsbrixham.co.uk**

Self-catering
West Banbury Farm Cottages,
BROADWOODWIDGER, Lifton,
Devon PL16 0JJ
Tel: 01566 780423
• **e-mail:**
westbanburnyfarm@btinternet.com
• **website: www.westbanbury.co.uk**

Farm / Self-Catering / B&B
Mrs Lee, Church Approach Cottages,
Church Green, Farway, COLYTON, Devon
EX24 6EQ
Tel: 01404 871383/871202
• **e-mail: lizlee@eclipse.co.uk**
• **website: www.churchapproach.co.uk**

Self-catering
Linda & Jim Watt, Northcote Manor
Farm Holiday Cottages, Kentisbury,
COMBE MARTIN, Devon EX31 4NB
Tel: 01271 882376
• **e-mail: info@northcotemanorfarm.co.uk**
• **website: www.northcotemanorfarm.co.uk**

Guest House
Overcombe House, Old Station Road,
Horrabridge, Yelverton, DARTMOOR,
Devon PL20 7RA
Tel: 01822 853501
• **e-mail: enquiries@overcombehotel.co.uk**
• **website: www.overcombehotel.co.uk**

Self-Catering
Christine Clark, Dart Valley Cottages,
Parklands, Dartmouth Road, Stoke Fleming,
DARTMOUTH, Devon TQ6 0QY.
Tel: 01803 771127
• **e-mail. enquiries@dartvalleycottages.co.uk**
• **website: www.dartvalleycottages.co.uk**

Self-Catering / Holiday Park
Cofton Country Holidays, Starcross, Near
DAWLISH, Devon EX6 8RP
Tel: 0800 085 8649
• **website: www.coftonholidays.co.uk**

Inn
The Blue Ball Inn, Countisbury, LYNMOUTH,
Near Lynton, Devon EX35 6NE
Tel: 01598 741263
• **website: www.BlueBallinn.com**
                  www.exmoorsandpiper.com

Self-Catering
G Davidson Richmond, Clooneavin,
Clooneavin Path, LYNMOUTH, Devon
EX35 6EE • Tel: 01598 753334
• **e-mail: relax@clooneavinholidays.co.uk**
• **website: www.clooneavinholidays.co.uk**

B & B
Merritt House, 7 Queens Road,
PAIGNTON, Devon TQ4 6AT
• e-mail: bookings@merritthouse.com
• website: www.merritthouse.co.uk

Hotel / Inn / Self Catering
Port Light Hotel & Bolberry Farm Cottages,
Bolberry Down, Near SALCOMBE, Devon
TQ7 3DY • Tel: 01548 561384
• e-mail: info@portlight.co.uk
• website: www.portlight.co.uk
            www.bolberryfarmcottages.co.uk

Guest House
A J Hill, Beaumont, Castle Hill, SEATON
Devon EX12 2QW
Tel: 01297 20832
• e-mail: tony@lymebay.demon.co.uk
• website:
www.smoothhound.co.uk/hotels/beaumon1.html

Holiday / Caravan Park
Oakdown Holiday Park, Weston,
SIDMOUTH, Devon, EX10 0PT
Tel: 01297 680387
• e-mail: enquiries@oakdown.co.uk
• website: www.oakdown.co.uk

Caravans / Camping
Salcombe Regis Camping & Caravan
Park, SIDMOUTH, Devon EX10 0JH
Tel: 01395 514303
• e-mail: contact@salcombe-regis.co.uk
• website: www.salcombe-regis.co.uk

Self-Catering / Camping
Dartmoor Country Holidays, Magpie Leisure
Park, Bedford Bridge, Horrabridge,
Yelverton, TAVISTOCK, Devon PL20 7RY
Tel: 01822 852651
• website: www.dartmoorcountryholidays.co.uk

Guest House
Hampton Manor, Alston, Callington,
Near TAVISTOCK, Cornwall PL17 8LX
Tel: 01579 370494
• email: hamptonmanor@supanet.com
• website: www.hamptonmanor.co.uk

Caravan / Camping Park
Harford Bridge Holiday Park, Peter Tavy,
TAVISTOCK, Devon PL19 9LS
Tel: 01822 810349
• email: enquiry@harfordbridge.co.uk
• website: www.harfordbridge.co.uk

Holiday Park
Longstone Manor Holiday Park,
Moortown, TAVISTOCK,
Devon PL19 9JZ
Tel: 01822 613371
• e-mail: web@langstonemanor.co.uk
• website: www.langstonemanor.co.uk

B&B
Sampford Manor, Sampford Spiney,
Yelverton, TAVISTOCK, Devon PL20 6LH
Tel: 01822 853442
• e-mail:
manor@sampford-spiney.fsnet.co.uk
• website:
www.sampford-spiney.fsnet.co.uk

Guest House
Diane Shelton, Avron House, 70
Windsor Road, TORQUAY TQ1 1SZ
Tel: 01803 294182
• e-mail: arronhouse@blueyonder.co.uk
• website: www.avronhouse.co.uk

Hotel
Riviera Lodge Hotel, 26 Croft Road.
TORQUAY, Devon TQ2 5UE
Tel: 01803 209309
• e-mail: stay@rivieralodgehotel.co.uk
• website: www.rivieralodgehotel.co.uk

Self-catering
Cloister Park Cottages, Frithelstock,
TORRINGTON, Devon EX38 8JH
Tel: 01805 622518
• website : www.cloisterpark.co.uk

Holiday Park
Woolacombe Bay Holiday Parks,
WOOLACOMBE, Devon
Tel: 0844 770 0384
• website: www.woolacombe.com

Caravan & Camping
North Morte Farm Caravan & Camping Park,
Mortehoe, WOOLACOMBE, Devon EX34 7EG
Tel: 01271 870381
• e-mail: info@northmortefarm.co.uk
• website: www.northmortefarm.co.uk

•DORSET

Hotel
Southbourne Grove Hotel, 96 Southbourne
Road, BOURNEMOUTH, Dorset BH6 3QQ
Tel: 01202 420503
• e-mail: neil@pack1462.freeserve.co.uk
• website: www.southbournegrovehotel.co.uk

Self-Catering
C. Hammond, Stourcliffe Court, 56
Stourcliffe Avenue, Southbourne,
BOURNEMOUTH, Dorset BH6 3PX
Tel: 01202 420698
• e-mail: rjhammond1@hotmail.co.uk
• website: www.stourcliffecourt.co.uk

Self-Catering Cottage / Farmhouse B & B
Mrs C. L. Norman, Frogmore Farm,
Chideock, BRIDPORT, Dorset DT6 0HT
Tel: 01308 456159
• e-mail: bookings@frogmorefarm.com
• website: www.frogmorefarm.com

Self-catering
Lancombes House, West Milton,
BRIDPORT, Dorset, DT6 3TN
Tel: 01308 485375
• e-mail: info@lancombes-house.co.uk
• website: www.lancombes-house.co.uk

Self-Catering
Josephine Pearse, Tamarisk Farm Cottages,
Beach Road, West Bexington,
DORCHESTER, Dorset DT2 9DF
Tel: 01308 897784
• e-mail: holidays@tamariskfarm.com
• website: www.tamariskfarm.com/holidays

Farmhouse B&B
Luckford Wood Farmhouse, Church
Street, Easte Stoke, Wareham, Near
LULWORTH, Dorset BH20 6AW
Tel: 01929 463098
• e-mail: luckfordleisure@hotmail.co.uk
• website: www.luckfordleisure.co.uk

Self-Catering
Westover Farm Cottages, Wootton Fitzpaine,
Near LYME REGIS, Dorset DT6 6NE
Tel: 01297 560451/561395
• e-mail: wfcottages@aol.com
• website: www.westoverfarmcottages.co.uk

Self-Catering
Mrs E Melville, Wood Dairy, Wood Lane,
NORTH PERROTT, Somerset/Dorset
TA18 7TA
Tel: 01935 891532
• e-mail: liz@acountryretreat.co.uk
• website: www.acountryretreat.co.uk

Golf Lodge / Hotel
The Dorset Golf & Country Club, Hyde,
Bere Regis, Near POOLE,
Dorset BH20 7NT
Tel: 01929 472244
• e-mail: admin@dorsetgolfresort.com
• website: www.dorsetgolfresort.com

Caravan Park
Axedale Caravan Park, Colyford Road,
SEATON, Devon EX12 2DF
• e-mail: info@axevale.co.uk
• website: www.axevale.co.uk

Hotel
The Knoll House, STUDLAND BAY,
Dorset BH19 3AW
Tel: 01929 450450
• e-mail: info@knollhouse.co.uk
• website: www.knollhouse.co.uk

Inn B&B
The White Swan, The Square, 31 High
Street, SWANAGE BN19 2LJ
Tel: 01929 423804
• e-mail: info@whiteswanswanage.co.uk
• website: www.whiteswanswanage.co.uk

•DURHAM

Golf Club
Brancepeth Castle Golf Club,
Brancepeth, DURHAM DH7 8EA
Tel: 0191 378 0075
• e-mail: enquiries@brancepeth-castle-golf.co.uk
• website: www.brancepeth-castle-golf.co.uk

•GLOUCESTERSHIRE

Hotel
Tudor Farmhouse Hotel, CLEARWELL,
Forest of Dean, Gloucs GL16 8JS
Tel: 01594 833046
• e-mail: info@tudorfarmhousehotel.co.uk
• website: www.tudorfarmhousehotel.co.uk

Guest House
Mr John Sparrey, Parkview Guest House, 4
Pittville Crescent, CHELTENHAM, Gloucs
GL52 2QZ
Tel: 01242 575567
• e-mail: stay@parkviewguesthouse.me.uk
• website: www.parkviewguesthouse.me.uk

Self-catering
Orion Holidays, COTSWOLDS, South
Cerney
Tel: 01285 861839
• e-mail: contact@orionholidays.com
• website: www.orionholidays.com

Please mention this FHG
Guide when enquiring
about accommodation
featured in these pages

Self-Catering
Two Springbank, 37 Hopton Road, Cam,
DURSLEY, Gloucs GL11 5PD
Contact: Mrs F A Jones, 32 Everlands, Cam,
Dursley, Gloucs G11 5NL
Tel: 01453 543047
• e-mail: info@twospringbank.co.uk
• website: www.twospringbank.co.uk

Guest House
Elizabeth Warland, Hambutts Mynd, Edge
Road, PAINSWICK, Gloucs GL6 6UP
Tel: 01452 812352
• e-mail: ewarland@supanet.com.
• website:
www.accommodation.uk.net/painswick.htm

Self-Catering
Nicky Cross, Wharton Lodge Cottages,
Weston-Under-Penyard, ROSS-ON-WYE,
Forest of Dean, Gloucs HR9 7JX
Tel: 01989 750140
• e-mail: ncross@whartonlodge.co.uk
• website: www.whartonlodge.co.uk

Hotel
The Old Stocks Hotel, Restaurant & Bar,
The Square, STOW-ON-THE-WOLD,
Gloucestershire GL54 1AF
Tel: 01451 830666
• e-mail: fhg@oldstockshotel.co.uk
• website: www.oldstockshotel.co.uk

B & B
Mrs A Rhoton, Hyde Crest, Cirencester Road,
Minchinhampton, STROUD, Gloucs GL6 8PE
Tel: 01453 731631
• e-mail: stay@hydecrest.co.uk
• website: www.hydecrest.co.uk

• HAMPSHIRE

Hotel / Inn
The Three Lions, Stuckton,
FORDINGBRIDGE, Hampshire SP6 2HF
Tel: 01425 652489
• e-mail: the3lions@btinternet.com
• website:
www.thethreelionsrestaurant.co.uk

Holiday Park
Downton Holiday Park, Shorefield Road,
Milford-on-Sea, NEW FOREST, Hampshire
SO41 0LH
Tel: 01425 476131 / 01590 642515
• e-mail: info@downtonholidaypark.co.uk
• website: www.downtonholidaypark.co.uk

Touring / Camping
Red Shoot Camping Park, Linwood,
RINGWOOD, Hampshire BH24 3QT
Tel: 01425 473789
• e-mail:
enquiries@redshoot-campingpark.com
• website: www.redshoot-campingpark.com

• HEREFORDSHIRE

Self-catering
Mrs C.Williams, Radnor's End,
Huntington, KINGTON, Herefordshire
HR5 3NZ
Tel: 01544 370289
• e-mail: enquiries@the-rock-cottage.co.uk
• website: www.the-rock-cottage.co.uk

Self-catering
Cowarne Hall Cottages, MUCH
COWARNE, Herefordshire HR7 4JQ
Tel: 01432 820317
• e-mail: rm@cowarnehall.co.uk
• website: www.cowarnehall.co.uk

Hotel
Chasedale Hotel, Walford Road, ROSS-
ON-WYE, Herefordshire HR9 5PQ
Tel: 01989 562423
• e-mail: chasedale@supanet.com
• website: www.chasedale.co.uk

• KENT

Hotel
The Hanson, 41 Belvedere Road,
BROADSTAIRS, Kent CT10 1PF
Tel: 01843 868936
• e-mail: hotel.hanson@yahoo.co.uk
• website: www.hansonhotel.co.uk

Self-Catering
Mr A Vincent, Golding Hop Farm, Bewley
Lane, Plaxtol, SEVENOAKS, Kent TN15 0PS
Tel: 07771 520229
• e-mail: info@goldinghopfarm.com
• website: www.goldinghopfarm.com

Guest House
Mrs S.Twort, Heron Cottage, Biddenden,
TENTERDEN, Near Ashford, Kent
TN27 8HH
Tel: 01580 291358
• e-mail: susantwort@hotmail.com
• website: www.heroncottage.info

•LANCASHIRE

Guest House
Parr Hall Farm, Parr Lane, Eccleston,
CHORLEY, Lancs PR7 5SL
Tel: 01257 451917
• e-mail: enquiries@parrhallfarm.com
  website: www.parrhallfarm.com

•LINCOLNSHIRE

Lodges / Touring Caravan Park
Mr & Mrs A Potts, Walnut Lake Lodges &
Camping Park, Main Road, Algarkirk,
BOSTON, Lincs PE20 2LQ
Tel: 01205 460482
• e-mail: mariawalnutlakes@yahoo.co.uk
• website: www.walnutlakes.co.uk

Self Catering / Touring Caravan Park
Woodland Waters, Willoughby Road,
Ancaster, GRANTHAM NE32 3RT
Tel: 01400 230888
• e-mail: info@woodlandwaters.co.uk
• website: www.woodlandwaters.co.uk

Self Catering
Mr A Tuxworth, Poachers Hideaway Holiday
Cottages, Flintwood Farm, Belchford,
HORNCASTLE, Lincolnshire LN9 5QN
Tel: 01507 533555
• e-mail: info@poachershideaway.com
• website: www.poachershideaway.com

Self-catering
Paul & Flora Bennett, Butterdon Hall
Coach Haise Holidays, LOUTH,
Lincolnshire LN11 0NS
Tel: 01507 603193
• e-mail:
paulandflora@brackenboroughhall.com
• website: www.brackenboroughhall.com

B & B
Mrs Hodgkinson, Kirkstead Oldmill Cottage,
Tattershall Road, WOODHALL SPA,
Lincolnshire LN10 6UQ
Tel: 01526 353637
• e-mail: barbara@woodhallspa.com
• website: www.woodhallspa.com

•NORFOLK

Holiday Park
Castaways Holiday Park, Paston Road,
BACTON-ON-SEA, Norfolk NR12 0JB
Tel : 01692 650436
• e-mail: info@castawaysholidaypark.net
• website: www.castawaysholidaypark.net

Hotel
The Hoste Arms, The Green, BURNHAM
MARKET, Norfolk PE31 8HD
Tel: 01328 738777
• e-mail: reception@hostearms.co.uk
• website: www.hostearms.co.uk

Holiday Park
Waveney Valley Holiday Park, Airstation
Lane, Rushall, DISS, Norfolk IP21 4QF
Tel: 01379 741228
• e-mail: waveneyvalleyhp@aol.com
• website: www.caravanparksnorfolk.co.uk

Self-Catering
Blue Riband Holidays, HEMSBY,
Great Yarmouth, Norfolk NR29 4HA
Tel: 01493 730445
• website: www.BlueRibandHolidays.co.uk

Hotel
The Stuart House Hotel, 35 Goodwins Road,
KING'S LYNN, Norfolk PE30 5QX
Tel: 01553 772169
• e-mail: reception@stuarthousehotel.co.uk
• website: www.stuarthousehotel.co.uk
           www.stuart-house-hotel.co.uk

Self-catering
Scarning Dale, Dale Road, SCARNING,
Dereham, Norfolk NR19 2QN
Tel: 01362 687269
• e-mail: jean@scarningdale.co.uk
• website: www.scarningdale.co.uk

Self-Catering
Winterton Valley Holidays, Edward Road,
WINTERTON-ON-SEA, Norfolk NR29 4BX
Contact: 15 Kingston Avenue, Caister on
Sea, Norfolk NR30 5ET
Tel: 01493 377175
• e-mail: info@wintertonvalleyholidays.co.uk
• website: www.wintertonvalleyholidays.co.uk

•NORTHUMBERLAND

Self-catering
Point Cottages, BAMBURGH,
Northumberland
Contact : J&E Sanderson, 30 The Oval,
Benton, Newcastle-Upon-Tyne
NE12 9PP
Tel: 0191 2662800
• e-mail: info@bamburgh-cottages.co.uk
• website: www.bamburgh-cottages.co.uk

Self-catering
Bank House Holiday Cottages,
GUYZANCE, Northumberland NE65 9AP
Tel: 07957 100615
• e-mail:
info@bankhouseholidaycottages.co.uk
• website:
www.bankhouseholidaycottages.co.uk

Inn
The Bay Horse Inn, West Woodburn,
HEXHAM, Northumberland NE48 2RX
Tel: 01434 2710218
• e-mail: **enquiry@bayhorseinn.org**
• website: **www.bayhorseinn.org**

•NOTTINGHAMSHIRE

B & B
The Grange Bed & Breakfast, Sutton
Lane, ELTON, Notts NG13 9LA
Tel: 07887 952181
• website:
www.thegrangebedandbreakfastnotts.co.uk

Caravan & Camping Park
Orchard Park, Marnham Road, Tuxford,
NEWARK, Nottinghamshire NG22 0PY
Tel: 01777 870228
• e-mail: **info@orchardcaravanpark.co.uk**
• website: **www.orchardcaravanpark.co.uk**

•OXFORDSHIRE

B & B / Guest House
June Collier, Colliers, 55 Nethercote Road,
Tackley, KIDLINGTON, Oxfordshire OX5 3AT
Tel: 01869 331255 / 07790 338225
• e-mail: **junecollier@btinternet.com**
• website: **www.colliersbnb.co.uk**

Guest House
The Bungalow, Cherwell Farm, Mill
Lane, Old Mawston, OXFORD OX3 0QF
Tel: 01865 557171
• e-mail: **ros.bungalowbb@btinternet.com**
• website:
www.cherwellfarm-oxford-accom.co.uk

•SHROPSHIRE

Hotel
Longmynd Hotel, Cunnery Rd, CHURCH
STRETTON, Shropshire SY6 6AG
Tel. 01094 722244
• e-mail: **info@longmynd.co.uk**
• website: **www.longmynd.co.uk**

Self-Catering
Clive & Cynthia Prior, Mocktree Barns
Holiday Cottages, Leintwardine, LUDLOW,
Shropshire SY7 0LY
Tel: 01547 540441
• e-mail: **mocktreebarns@care4free.net**
• website: **www.mocktreeholidays.co.uk**

Self-Catering
Jane Cronin, Sutton Court Farm Cottages,
Sutton Court Farm, Little Sutton, LUDLOW,
Shropshire SY8 2AJ
Tel: 01584 861305
• e-mail: **enquiries@suttoncourtfarm.co.uk**
• website: **www.suttoncourtfarm.co.uk**

•SOMERSET

Farm / Guest House / Self-Catering
Jackie Bishop, Toghill House Farm, Freezing
Hill, Wick, Near BATH, Somerset BS30 5RT
Tel: 01225 891261
• e-mail:
accommodation@toghillhousefarm.co.uk
• website: **www.toghillhousefarm.co.uk**

B & B
Mrs C Bryson, Walton Villa, 3 Newbridge
Hill, BATH, Somerset BA1 3PW
Tel: 01225 482792
• e-mail: **walton.villa@virgin.net**
• website: **www.walton.izest.com**

Self-Catering
Westward Rise Holiday Park, South Road,
BREAN, Burnham-on-Sea, Somerset TA8 2RD
Tel: 01278 751310
• e-mail: **info@westwardrise.com**
• website: **www.westwardrise.com**

Caravan Park
Fairways Caravan Park, Bath Road,
Bawdrip, BRIDGEWATER, Somerset
TA7 8PP
Tel: 01278 685569
• e-mail:
holiday@fairwaysinternational.co.uk
• website: **www.fairwaysinternational.co.uk**

Farmhouse B&B
Mrs M Hasell, The Model Farm, Norton
Hawkfield, Pensford, BRISTOL
BS39 4HA
Tel: 01275 832144
• e-mail: **margarethasell@hotmail.com**
• website: **www.themodelfarm.co.uk**

FHG Guides

Hotel
Yarn Market Hotel, High Street,
DUNSTER, Somerset TA24 6SF
Tel: 01643 821425
- e-mail: **hotel@yarnmarkethotel.co.uk**
- website: **www.yarnmarkethotel.co.uk**

Self-catering / Camping
Westermill Farm, EXFORD, Exmoor,
Somerset TA24 7NJ
Tel: 01643 831238
- e-mail: **fhg@westermill.com**
- website: **www.westermill.com**

Self Catering
Mrs L M Garner, The Pack Horse, Allerford
Near Porlock, EXMOOR, Somerset TA24 8HW
Tel: 01643 862475
- e-mail: **holidays@thepackhorse.net**
- website: **www.thepackhorse.net**

Self-Catering / Holiday Park / Touring Pitches
Mary Randle, St Audries Bay Holiday Club,
MINEHEAD, Somerset TA4 4DA
Tel: 01984 632515
- e-mail: **info@staudriesbay.co.uk**
- website: **www.staudriesbay.co.uk**

Farm / B & B
North Down Farm, Pyncombe Lane,
Wiveliscombe, TAUNTON, Somerset TA4 2BL
Tel: 01984 623730
- e-mail: **jennycope@btinternet.com**
- website: **www.north-down-farm.co.uk**

B & B
The Old Mill, Netherclay, Bishop's Hull,
TAUNTON, Somerset TA1 5AB
Tel: 01823 289732
- website: www.theoldmillbandb.co.uk /
  www.bandbtaunton.co.uk

Farm / Guest House
G. Clark, Yew Tree Farm, THEALE,
Near Wedmore, Somerset BS28 4SN
Tel: 01934 712475
- e-mail: **enquiries@yewtreefarmbandb.co.uk**
- website: **www.yewtreefarmbandb.co.uk**

B & B
Mrs S Crane, Birdwood House, Bath Road,
WELLS, Somerset BA5 3EW
Tel: 01749 679250
- e-mail: **info@birdwood-bandb.co.uk**
- website: **www.birdwood-bandb.co.uk**

Guest House
Infield House, 36 Portway, WELLS,
Somerset BA5 2BN
Tel: 01749 670989
- e-mail: **infield@talk21.com**
- website: **www.infieldhouse.co.uk**

Self-catering
Somerset Court Cottages, Wick St
Lawrence, Near WESTON-SUPER-
MARE, Somerset BS22 7YR
Tel: 01934 521383
- e-mail:
  peter@somersetcourtcottages.co.uk
- website:
  www.somersetcourtcottages.co.uk

•STAFFORDSHIRE

Farm B & B / Self-Catering
Mrs M. Hiscoe-James, Offley Grove Farm,
Adbaston, ECCLESHALL, Staffs ST20 0QB
Tel: 01785 280205
- e-mail: **enquiries@offleygrovefarm.co.uk**
- website: **www.offleygrovefarm.co.uk**

Self-Catering
T.A. Mycock, Rosewood Cottage, Lower
Berkhamsytch, Bottom House, Near LEEK,
Staffordshire ST13 7QP
Tel: 01538 308213
- website: **www.rosewoodcottage.co.uk**

•SUFFOLK

B & B / Guest House
Dunston Guest House, 8 Springfield Road,
BURY ST EDMUNDS, Suffolk IP33 3AN
Tel: 01284 767981
- e-mail: **anndakin@btconnect.com**
- website: **www.dunstonguesthouse.co.uk**

Self-Catering
Kessingland Cottages, Rider Haggard Lane,
KESSINGLAND, Suffolk.
Contact: S. Mahmood, 156 Bromley Road,
Beckenham, Kent BR3 6PG
Tel: 020 8650 0539
- e-mail: **jeeptrek@kjti.co.uk**
- website: **www.k-cottage.co.uk**

Holiday Park
Broadland Holiday Village, Oulton
Broad, LOWESTOFT, Suffolk NR33 9JY
Tel: 01502 573033
- e-mail: **info@broadlandvillage.co.uk**
- website: **www.broadlandvillage.co.uk**

•SURREY

Self-Catering / B & B
Mrs J Howell, Little Orchard B & B, 152
London Road North, MERSTHAM,
Surrey RH1 3AA
Tel: 01737 558707
- e-mail:**jackie@littleorchardbandb.co.uk**
- website: **www.littleorchardbandb.co.uk**

•EAST SUSSEX

Hotel
Grand Hotel, 1 Grand Parade, St Leonards,
HASTINGS, East Sussex TN37 6AQ
Tel: 01424 428510
• e-mail: info@grandhotelhastings.co.uk
• website: www.grandhotelhastings.co.uk

B & B
Maon Hotel, 26 Upper Rock Gardens,
BRIGHTON, East Sussex BN2 1QE
Tel: 01273 694400
• e-mail: maonhotel@aol.com
• website: www.maonhotel.co.uk

Self-Catering
"Pekes", CHIDDINGLY, East Sussex
Contact: Eva Morris, 124 Elm Park
Mansions, Park Walk, London SW10 0AR
Tel: 020 7352 8088
• e-mail: pekes.afa@virgin.net
• website: www.pekesmanor.com

Guest House / Self-Catering
Longleys Farm Cottage, Harebeating Lane,
HAILSHAM, East Sussex BN27 1ER
Tel: 01323 841227
• e-mail: thestable@longleysfarmcottage.com
• website: www.longleysfarmcottage.co.uk

Hotel
Rye Lodge Hotel, Hilders Cliff, RYE, East
Sussex TN31 7LD
Tel: 01797 223838
• e-mail: info@ryelodge.co.uk
• website: www.ryelodge.co.uk

• WEST SUSSEX

B & B
Vicki Richards Woodacre, Arundel Road,
Fontwell, ARUNDEL, West Sussex
BN18 0QP
Tel: 01243 814301
• e-mail: wacrebb@aol.com
• website: www.woodacre.co.uk

Self-Catering
Mrs M. W. Carreck, New Hall Holiday Flat
and Cottage, New Hall Lane, Small Dole,
HENFIELD, West Sussex BN5 9YJ
Tel: 01273 492646
• e-mail: norman.carreck@btinternet.com
• website: www.newhallcottage.co.uk

B & B
Beacon Lodge Bed & Breakfast, London
Road, Watersfield, PULBOROUGH,
West Sussex RH20 1NH
Tel: 01798 831026
• website: www.beaconlodge.co.uk

Guest Accommodation
St Andrews Lodge, Chichester Road,
SELSEY, West Sussex PO20 0LX
Tel: 01243 606899
• e-mail: info@standrewslodge.co.uk
• website: www.standrewslodge.co.uk

•WARWICKSHIRE

Caravan Touring Park
Dodwell Park, Evesham Road, STRATFORD-
UPON-AVON, Warwickshire CV37 9SR
Tel: 01784 204957
• e-mail: enquiries@dodwellpark.co.uk
• website: www.dodwellpark.co.uk

Guest House
John & Julia Downie, Holly Tree
Cottage, Pathlow, STRATFORD-UPON-
AVON, Warwickshire CV37 0ES
Tel: 01789 204461
• e-mail: john@hollytree-cottage.co.uk
• website: www.hollytree-cottage.co.uk

•WORCESTERSHIRE

Self-Catering / B & B
Mrs Diane Mann, Pitlands Farm,
Clifton-on-Teme, WORCESTER, Worcs
WR6 6DX
Tel: 01886 812220
• e-mail: info@pitlandsfarm.co.uk
• website: www.pitlandsfarm.co.uk

•NORTH YORKSHIRE

Farmhouse B & B
Mrs Julie Clarke, Middle Farm, Woodale,
COVERDALE, Leyburn, North Yorkshire
DL8 4TY • Tel: 01969 640271
• e-mail: j-a-clarke@hotmail.co.uk
• www.yorkshirenet.co.uk/stayat/middlefarm/
index.htm

Farm
Mrs Linda Tindall, Rowantree Farm, Fryup
Road, Ainthorpe, DANBY, Whitby, North
Yorkshire YO21 2LE • Tel: 01287 660396
• e-mail: krbsatindall@aol.com
• website: www.rowantreefarm.co.uk

Self-catering
Rudding Holiday Park, Follifoot,
HARROGATE, North Yorkshire HG3 1JH
Tel: 01423 870439
• e-mail: stay@ruddingpark.com
• website: www.ruddingholidaypark.co.uk

Self-catering
Southfield Farm Holiday Cottages,
Darley, HARROGATE, North Yorkshire
HG3 2PR
Tel: 01423 780258
• e-mail: info@southfieldcottages.co.uk
• website: www.southfieldcottages.co.uk

Guest House
The New Inn Motel, Main Street, HUBY,
York, North Yorkshire YO61 1HQ
Tel: 01347 810219
• enquiries@newinnmotel.freeserve.co.uk
• website: www.newinnmotel.co.uk

Self-Catering
Mrs Jones, New Close Farm, KIRKBY
MALHAM, Skipton, North Yorkshire BD23 4DP
Tel: 01729 830240
• e-mail:
brendajones@newclosefarmyorkshire.co.uk
• website: www.newclosefarmyorkshire.co.uk

Self-Catering
Allaker in Coverdale, West Scrafton,
LEYBURN, North Yorkshire DL8 4RM
Contact: Mr Adrian Cave, 21 Kenilworth
Road, London W5 5PA Tel: 020 856 74862
• e-mail: ac@adriancave.com
• www.adriancave.com/allaker

Self-Catering
Abbey Holiday Cottages, MIDDLESMOOR
(Panorama Close, Halstey Bridge)
Harrogate, North Yorkshire HG3 5NY
Tel: 01423 712062
• e-mail: info@abbeyhallcottages.com
• website: www.fhgahcottages.com

Self-catering
East Farm Country Cottages, SCALBY
NABS, Scarborough, N.Yorkshire
YO13 0SL
Tel: 01723 353635
• e-mail: joeastfarmcottages@hotmail.co.uk
• website:
www.eastfarmcountrycottages.co.uk

Guest House / Self-Catering
Sue & Tony Hewitt, Harmony Country Lodge,
80 Limestone Road, Burniston,
SCARBOROUGH, North Yorkshire YO13 0DG
Tel: 0800 2985840
• e-mail: mail@harmonylodge.net
• website: www.harmonycountrylodge.co.uk

Self-catering
2 Hollies Cottages, Stainforth, SETTLE,
N.Yorkshire
Contact: Townhead Cottage, Stainforth,
Near Settle BD24 9PJ
Tel: 01729 822255
• website: www.stainforth-holiday-cottage-settle.co.uk

B & B
Beck Hall, Cove Road, Malham,
SKIPTON, N.Yorksire BD23 4DJ
Tel: 01729 830332
• e-mail: simon@beckhallmalham.com
• website: www.beckhallmalham.com

Hotel
The Coniston Hotel, Coniston Cold,
SKIPTON, North Yorkshire BD23 4EA
Tel: 01756 748080
• e-mail: info@theconistonhotel.com
• website: www.theconistonhotel.com

Self-Catering
York Lakeside Lodges Ltd, Moor Lane,
YORK, North Yorkshire YO24 2QU
Tel: 01904 702346
• e-mail: neil@yorklakesidelodges.co.uk
• website: www.yorklakesidelodges.co.uk

.SCOTLAND

•ANGUS & DUNDEE

Golf Club
Edzell Golf Club, High Street, EDZELL,
Brechin, Angus DD9 7TF
Tel: 01356 648462
• e-mail: **secretary@edzellgolfclub.net**
• website: **www.edzellgolfclub.net**

•ARGYLL & BUTE

Self-catering
Appin House Lodges, APPIN, Argyll
PA38 4BN
Tel: 01631 730207
• e-mail: **denys@appinhouse.co.uk**
• website: **www.appinhouse.co.uk**

Self-Catering
Ardtur Cottages, APPIN, Argyll PA38 4DD
Tel: 01631 730223
• e-mail: **pery@btinternet.com**
• website: **www.ardturcottages.com**

Self-Catering
Blarghour Farm Cottages, Blarghour Farm,
By Dalmally, INVERARAY, Argyll PA33 1BW
Tel: 01866 833246
• e-mail: **blarghour@btconnect.com**
• website: **www.self-catering-argyll.co.uk**

Self-catering
Brian & Mary Phillips, Kilbride Croft,
Balvicar, ISLE OF SEIL, Argyll PA34 4RD
Tel: 01852 300475
• e-mail: **kilbridecroft@aol.com**
• website: **www.kilbridecroft.co.uk**

Self-Catering
Inchmurrin Island Self-Catering Holidays,
Inchmurrin Island, LOCH LOMOND G63 0JY
Tel: 01389 850245
• e-mail: **scotts@inchmurrin-lochlomond.com**
• website: **www.inchmurrin-lochlomond.com**

Self-catering
West Coast Character Cottages, OBAN
Contact : J.Tricker, Tigh Beag, Connel,
Oban, Argyll PA37 1PJ
Tel: 01631 710504
• e-mail: **obanholidaycottages@talktalk.net**
• website: **www.obanholidaycottages.co.uk**

Self-Catering
Colin & Jo Mossman, Lagnakeil Highland
Lodges, Lerags, OBAN, Argyll PA34 4SE
Tel: 01631 562746
• e-mail: **info@lagnakeil.co.uk**
• website: **www.lagnakeil.co.uk**

Hotel
Falls of Lora Hotel, Connel Ferry, By OBAN,
Argyll PA37 1PB
Tel: 01631 710483
• e-mail: **enquiries@fallsoflora.com**
• website: **www.fallsoflora.com**

•AYRSHIRE & ARRAN

Farmhouse / B & B
Mrs Nancy Cuthbertson, West Tannacrieff,
Fenwick, KILMARNOCK, Ayrshire KA3 6AZ
Tel: 01560 600258
• e-mail: **westtannacrieff@btopenworld.com**
• website: **www.smoothhound.co.uk/hotels/
westtannacrieff.html**

•BORDERS

B & B
Hundalee House, JEDBURGH,
Roxburghshire TD8 6PA
Tel: 01835 863011
• e-mail: **sheila.whittaker@btinternet.com**
• website: **www.accommodation-
scotland.org**

Self-catering
Mill House, Near JEDBURGH,
Roxburghshire
Contact : Mrs A.Fraser, Overwells,
Jedburgh TD8 6LT
Tel: 01835 863020
• e-mail: **abfraser@btinternet.com**
• website: **www.overwells.co.uk**

B & B
The Garden House, Whitmuir, SELKIRK,
Borders TD7 4PZ
Tel: 01750 721728
• e-mail: **whitmuir@btconnect.com**
• website: **www.whitmuirfarm.co.uk**

**Please mention this
FHG Guide when enquiring
about accommodation
featured in these pages**

• DUMFRIES & GALLOWAY

Self-Catering
Barend Holiday Village, Barend Farmhouse, SANDYHILLS, Dalbeattie, Dumfries & Galloway DG5 4NU
Tel: 01387 780663
• e-mail: info@barendholidayvillage.co.uk
• website: www.barendholidayvillage.co.uk

Self-Catering
Ae Farm Cottages, Gubhill Farm, Ae, DUMFRIES, Dumfriesshire DG1 1RL
Tel: 01387 860648
• e-mail: gill@gubhill.co.uk
• website: www.aefarmcottages.co.uk

Farm / Camping & Caravans / Self-Catering
Barnsoul Farm Holidays, Barnsoul Farm, Shawhead, DUMFRIES, Dumfriesshire DG2 9SQ. Tel: 01387 730249
• e-mail: barnsouldg@aol.com
• website: www.barnsoulfarm.co.uk

Self-Catering
Rusko, GATEHOUSE OF FLEET, Castle Douglas, Dumfriesshire DG7 2BS
Tel: 01557 814215
• e-mail: info@ruskoholidays.co.uk
• website: www.ruskoholidays.co.uk

Hotel
Corsewall Lighthouse Hotel, Kirkcolm, STRANRAER, Dumfries & Galloway DG9 0QG
Tel: 01776 853220
• e-mail info@lighthousehotel.co.uk
• website: www.lighthousehotel.co.uk

• EDINBURGH & LOTHIANS

Guest House
Castle Park Guest House, 75 Gilmore Place, EDINBURGH EH3 9NU
Tel: 0131 229 1215
• e-mail: castlepark@btconnect.com
• website: www.castleparkguesthouse.co.uk

Guest House
International Guest House, 37 Mayfield Gardens, EDINBURGH EH9 2BX
Tel: 0131 667 2511
• e-mail: intergh1@yahoo.co.uk
• website: www.accommodation-edinburgh.com

Self-Catering
Mrs C. M. Kilpatrick, Slipperfield House, WEST LINTON, Peeblesshire EH46 7AA
Tel: 01968 660401
• e-mail: cottages@slipperfield.com
• website: www.slipperfield.com

• FIFE

Guest House
The Spindrift Guest House, Pittenweem Road, ANSTRUTHER, Fife KY10 3DT
Tel: 01333 310573
• e-mail: info@thespindrift.co.uk
• website: www.thespindrift.co.uk

Self-Catering
Pitcairlie Holiday Apartments, Pitcairlie House, AUCHTERMUCHTY, Fife KY14 6EU
Tel:01337 827418
• e-mail: reservations@pitcairlie-leisure.co.uk
• website: www.pitcairlie-leisure.co.uk

Hotel
Meldrums Hotel, 56 Main Street, Ceres, By Cupar, ST ANDREWS, Fife KY15 5NA
Tel: 01334 828286
• e-mail: meldrums@btconnect.com
• website: www.meldrums-hotel.co.uk

• HIGHLANDS

Self-catering
Islands & Highlands Cottages, Bridge Road, Portree, Isle of Skye IV51 9ER
Tel: 01478 612123
• e-mail: sales@islands-and-highlands.co.uk
• website: www.islands-and-highlands.co.uk

Self-Catering
Frank & Juliet Spencer-Nairn, Culligran Cottages, Struy, Near BEAULY, Inverness-shire IV4 7JX . Tel: 01463 761285
• e mail: info@culligranoottages.oo.uk
• website: www.culligrancottages.igne.co.uk

Self-Catering
Tyndrum, BOAT OF GARTEN, Inverness-shire Contact: Mrs Naomi C. Clark, Dochlaggie, Boat of Garten PH24 3BU
Tel: 01479 831242
• e-mail: dochlaggie99@aol.com

Self-Catering
Carol Hughes, Glenurquhart Lodges, Balnain, DRUMNADROCHIT, Inverness-shire IV63 6TJ
Tel: 01456 476234
• e-mail: carol@glenurquhartlodges.co.uk
• website: www.glenurquhart-lodges.co.uk

Hotel
The Clan MacDuff Hotel, Achintore Road, FORT WILLIAM, Inverness-shire PH33 6RW
Tel: 01397 702341
• e-mail: reception@clanmacduff.co.uk
• website: www.clanmacduff.co.uk

Caravan Park
A.J.Davis, Gruinard Bay Caravan Park,
LAIDE, Ross-shire IV22 2ND
Tel: 01445 731225
• website: www.gruinard.scotshost.co.uk

Hotel
Whitebridge Hotel, Whitebridge, LOCH
NESS, Inverness-shire IV2 6UN
Tel: 01456 486226
• e-mail: info@whitebridgehotel.co.uk
• website: www.whitebridgehotel.co.uk

B & B / Self-catering
Mondhuie Chalets & B&B, NETHY
BRIDGE, Inverness-shire PH25 3DF
Tel: 01479 821062
• e-mail: david@mondhuie.com
• website: www.mondhuie.com

B & B
Bruach Ard, POOLEWE
Tel: 01445 781765
• e-mail: dgeorge@globalnet.co.uk
• website: www.davidgeorge.co.uk

Self-Catering
Mr & Mrs S Dennis, Riverside Lodges,
Invergloy, SPEAN BRIDGE, Inverness-shire
PH34 4DY • Tel: 01397 712684
• e-mail: enquiries@riversidelodge.org.uk
• website: www.riversidelodge.org.uk

Self Catering
Broomview & Sunset Cottages, Rhiroy,
Lochbroom, By Garve, ULLAPOOL,
Ross-shire IV23 2QR
Contact: Mrs L Renwick, Spindrift, Keppoch
Farm, Dundonnell, Ross-shire IV23 2QR
Tel: 01854 633269
• e-mail: linda@lochbroomcottages.co.uk
• website: www.lochbroomcottages.co.uk

• LANARKSHIRE

Caravan & Holiday Home Park
Mount View Caravan Park, Station Road,
ABINGTON, South Lanarkshire ML12 6RW
Tel: 01864 502808
• e-mail: info@mountviewcaravanpark.co.uk
• website: www.mountviewcaravanpark.co.uk

• PERTH & KINROSS

Self-Catering
Loch Tay Lodges, Remony, Acharn,
ABERFELDY, Perthshire PH15 2HR
Tel: 01887 830209
• e-mail: remony@btinternet.com
• website: www.lochtaylodges.co.uk

Self-Catering
Laighwood Holidays, Laighwood,
DUNKELD, Perthshire PH8 0HB
Tel: 01350 724241
• e-mail: holidays@laighwood.co.uk
• website: www.laighwood.co.uk

Self- Catering
Atholl Cottage, Killiecrankie, PITLOCHRY,
Perthshire PH16 5LR
Contact: Mrs Joan Troup, Dalnasgadh,
Killiecrankie, Pitlochry, Perthshire PH16 5LN
Tel: 01796 470017
• e-mail: info@athollcottage.co.uk
• website: www.athollcottage.co.uk

Caravan Park
Milton of Fonab Caravan Park, Bridge
Road, PITLOCHRY, Perthshire PH16 5NA
Tel: 01796 472882
• e-mail: info@fonab.co.uk
• website: www.fonab.co.uk

• ORKNEY

Caravan & Camping
Pickaquoy Centre, KIRKWALL, Orkney
Tel: 01856 879900
• e-mail: enquiries@pickaquoy.com
• website: www.pickaquoy.co.uk

Caravan & Camping
Point of Ness, STROMNESS, Orkney
Tel: 01856 873535
• e-mail: recreation@orkney.gov.uk
• website: www.orkney.gov.uk

Hotel
Pierowall Hotel, WESTRAY, Orkney
KW17 2BZ
Tel: 01857 677472
• e-mail: enquiries@pierowallhotel.co.uk
• website: www.pierowallhotel.co.uk

FHG Guides publish a large range of well-known
accommodation guides. We will be happy to send you details
or you can use the order form at the back of this book.

•WALES

•ANGLESEY & GWYNEDD

Self-Catering

Crugeran Farm Holidays, ABERSOCH
Contact : Mrs R Parry, Crugeran, Sarn
Mellteyrn, Pwllheli, Gwynedd
LL53 8DT
Tel: 01758 730375
• **e-mail: post@crugeran.com**
• **website: www.crugeran.com**

Caravan Park

Islawrffordd Caravan Park, Tal-y-Bont,
BARMOUTH, Gwynedd LL43 2BQ
• **e-mail: info@islawrffordd.co.uk**
• **website: www.islawrffordd.co.uk**

Self-Catering / Caravan Site

Bryn Gloch Caravan and Camping Park,
Betws Garmon, CAERNARFON, Gwynedd
LL54 7YY Tel: 01286 650216
• **e-mail: eurig@bryngloch.co.uk**
• **website: www.bryngloch.co.uk**

Self-Catering Chalet

Chalet at Glan Gwna Holiday Park, Caethro,
CAERNARFON, Gwynedd
Contact: Mr H A Jones, Menai Bridge,
Caernarfon, Gwynedd LL59 5LN
Tel: 01248 712045
• **e-mail: hajones@northwales-chalet.co.uk**
• **website: www.northwales-chalet.co.uk**

Self-Catering

Pare Wernol, Chwilog Fawr, Chwilog,
Pwllheli, CRICCIETH, Gwynedd LL53 6SW
Tel: 01766 810506
• **website: www.wernol.co.uk**

Motel

The Beach Motel, Lon St Ffraid,
Trearddur Bay, HOLYHEAD, Anglesey
LL65 2YT
• **e-mail: info@thebeachmotel.co.uk**
• **website: www.thebeachmotel.co.uk**

Guest House

Cefn Uchaf Farm Guesthouse,
Garndolbenmaen, PORTHMADOG
Tel: 01766 530239
• **e-mail: enquiries@cefnuchaf.co.uk**
• **website: www.cefnuchaf.com**

Self-Catering

Mrs E A Williams, Tyddyn Heilyn, Chwilog,
PWLLHELI, Gwynedd LL53 6SW
Tel: 01766 810441
• **e-mail: tyddyn.heilyn@tiscali.co.uk**

Farm B&B

Mrs H Pugh, Pendre, Llanfihangel,
TYWYN, Gwynedd LL36 9UP
Tel: 01654 782385
• **e-mail: hugh.pugh01@btinternet.com**

•NORTH WALES

Guest House

Park Hill/Gwesty Bryn Parc, Llanrwst Road,
BETWS-Y-COED, Conwy LL24 0HD
Tel: 01690 710510
• **e-mail: welcome@park-hill.co.uk**
• **website: www.park-hill.co.uk**

Self-catering

Bron-Y-Wendon & Nant-Y-Glyn Holiday
Parks, Wern Road,Handdulas, COLWYN
BAY, North Wales LL22 8HG
Tel: 01492 512903/512282
• **e-mail: stay@northwales-holidays.co.uk**
• **website: www.northwales-holidays.co.uk**

Guest House

Mr D E Morgan, The Northwood, Rhos
Road, Rhos-on-Sea, COLWYN BAY, Conwy
LL28 4RS
Tel: 08450 533105
• **e-mail: welcome@thenorthwood.co.uk**
• **website: www.thenorthwood.co.uk**

• PEMBROKESHIRE

Self-catering

Llanteglos Estate, Llanteg, Near
AMROTH, Pembs SA67 8PU
• **e-mail: llanteglosestate@supanet.com**
• **website: www.llanteglos-estate.com**

Self-Catering

Timberhill Farm, BROAD HAVEN,
Pembrokeshire SA62 3LZ
Contact: Mrs L Ashton, 10 St Leonards
Road, Thames Ditton, Surrey KT7 0RJ
Tel: 02083 986349
• **e-mail: lejash@aol.com**
• **website: www.33timberhill.com**

www.holidayguides.com

Hotel
Michael & Suzy Beales, Castell Malgwyn
Hotel, LLechryd, CARDIGAN, Pembrokeshire
SA43 2QA
Tel: 01239 682382
• e-mail: reception@malgwyn.co.uk
• website: www.castellmalgwyn.co.uk

Self-Catering
Quality Cottages, Cerbid, Solva,
HAVERFORDWEST, Pembrokeshire SA62 6YE
Tel: 01348 837871
• e-mail: reserve@qualitycottages.co.uk
• website: www.qualitycottages.co.uk

Self-catering
Tynewydd Cottages, MOYLEGROVE,
Pembrokeshire
Tel: 01239 881280
• e-mail:
jaybillimoria@jaybillimoria.demon.co.uk

Self-catering
Ffynnon Ddofn, Llanon, Llanrhian, Near ST
DAVIDS, Pembrokeshire.
Contact: Mrs B. Rees White, Brick House
Farm, Burnham Road, Woodham Mortimer,
Maldon, Essex CM9 6SR. Tel: 01245 224611
• e-mail: daisypops@madasafish.com
• website: www.ffynnonddofn.co.uk

Farm Guest House
Mrs M. Jones, Lochmeyler Farm, Pen-Y-
Cwm, Near Solva, ST DAVIDS,
Pembrokeshire SA62 6LL
Tel: 01348 837724
• e-mail: stay@lochmeyler.co.uk
• website: www.lochmeyler.co.uk

Self-Catering
Mrs M. Pike, Porthiddy Farm Holiday
Cottages, Abereiddy, ST DAVIDS,
Pembrokeshire SA62 6DR
Tel: 01348 831004
• e-mail: m.pike@porthiddy.com
• website: www.porthiddy.com

•POWYS

Self-Catering
Old Stables Cottage & Old Dairy, Lane Farm,
Paincastle, Builth Wells, HAY-ON-WYE,
Powys LD2 3JS
Tel: 01497 851 605
• e-mail: lanefarm@onetel.com
• website: www.lane-farm.co.uk

Inn
Baskervill Arms Hotel, Clyro, HAY-ON-
WYE, Herefordshire HR3 5RZ
Tel: 01497 820670
• e-mail: bookings@baskervillearms.co.uk
• website: www.baskervillearms.co.uk

•SOUTH WALES

Campsite
Mr G. Watkins, Wernddu Caravan Park, Old
Ross Road, ABERGAVENNY,
Monmouthshire NP7 8NG
Tel:01873 856223
• e-mail: info@wernddu-golf-club.co.uk
• website: www.wernddu-golf-club.co.uk

•NORTHERN IRELAND

Caravan Park
Six Mile Water Carvan Park, Lough
Road, ANTRIM BT41 4DG
Tel: 028 9446 4963
• e-mail: sixmilewater@antrim.gov.uk
• website: www.antrim.gov.uk/caravanpark

Index of Towns and Counties

Accommodation Standards: Star Grading Scheme

The AA, VisitBritain, VisitScotland, and the VisitWales now use a single method of assessing and rating serviced accommodation. Irrespective of which organisation inspects an establishment the rating awarded will be the same, using a common set of standards, giving a clear guide of what to expect. They have full details of the grading system on their websites.

www.enjoyEngland.com

www.visitScotland.com

www.visitWales.com

www.theaa.com

Using a scale of 1-5 stars the objective quality ratings give a clear Indication of accommodation standard, cleanliness, ambience, hospitality, service and food.

This shows the full range of standards suitable for every budget and preference, and allows visitors to distinguish between the quality of accommodation and facilities on offer in different establishments.
All types of board and self-catering accommodation are covered, including hotels, B&Bs, holiday parks, campus accommodation, hostels, caravans and camping, and boats.

Gold and Silver awards are given to Hotels and Guest Accommodation that provide exceptional quality, especially in service and hospitality.

The more stars, the higher level of quality

★
acceptable quality; simple, practical, no frills

★★
good quality, well presented and well run

★★★
very good level of quality and comfort

★★★★
excellent standard throughout

★★★★★
exceptional quality, with a degree of luxury

National Accessible Scheme Logos for mobility impaired and older people

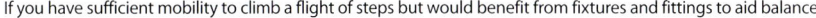

If you have particular mobility impairment. look out for the National Accessible Scheme. You can be confident of finding accommodation or attractions that meet your needs by looking for the following symbols.

Older and less mobile guests
If you have sufficient mobility to climb a flight of steps but would benefit from fixtures and fittings to aid balance.

Part-time wheelchair users
You have restricted walking ability or may need to use a wheelchair some of the time and can negotiate a maximum of 3 steps.

Independent wheelchair users
You are a wheelchair user and travel independently. Similar to the international logo for independent wheelchair users.

Assisted wheelchair users
You're a wheelchair user and travel with a friend or family member who helps you with everyday tasks.

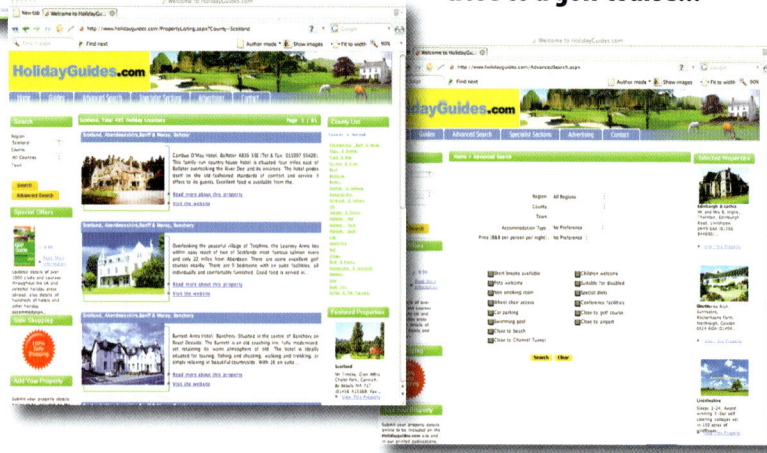

Other FHG titles for 2011

FHG Guides Ltd have been publishing an attractive range of
day accommodation guides for over 50 years. For all kinds of holiday
opportunities, they make useful gifts at any time of year.
guides are available in most bookshops and larger newsagents but
we will be happy to post you a copy direct If you have any difficulty.
POST FREE for addresses in the UK.
will also post abroad but have to charge separately for post or freight.

500
Great Places to Stay
in Britain
• Coast & Country Holidays
• Full range of family
accommodation

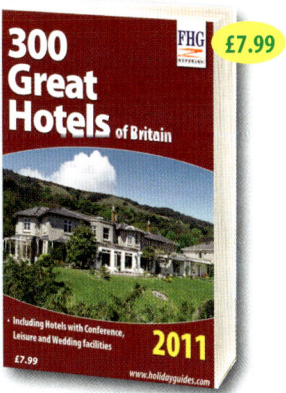

300
Great Hotels
of Britain
• Quality Hotels which offer the
best of traditional hospitality and
comfort

The Original
Pets Welcome!
• The bestselling guide to holidays
for pets and their owners

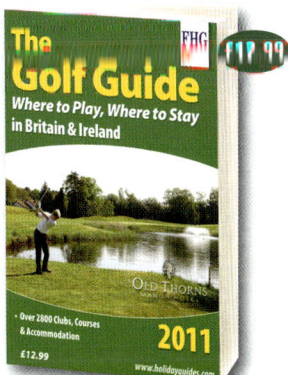

The Golf Guide
Where to Play, Where to Stay
• Approximately 2800 golf courses
in Britain and Ireland plus details
of convenient accommodation.

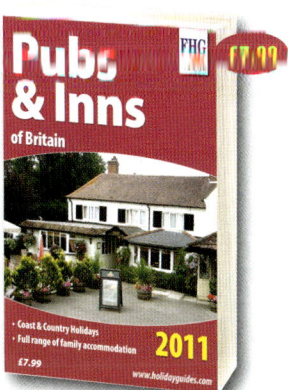

Pubs & Inns
of Britain
• Including Dog-friendly Pubs
• Accommodation, food and
traditional good cheer

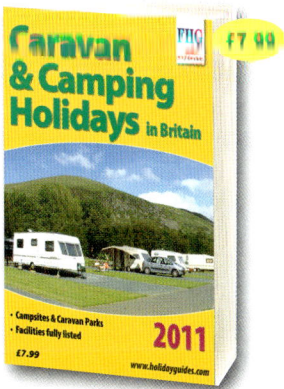

Caravan
& Camping Holidays
in Britain
• Campsites and Caravan parks
• Facilities fully listed

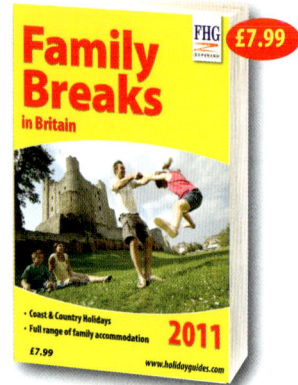

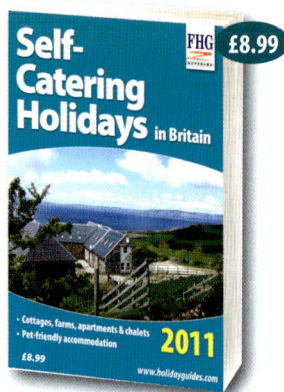

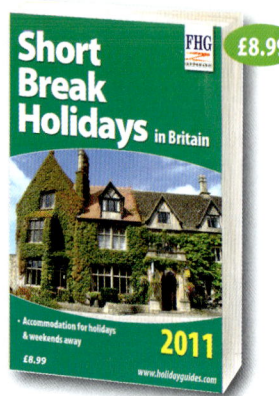

Family Breaks ☐
in Britain
• Accommodation, attractions and resorts
• Suitable for those with children and babies

Self-Catering Holidays ☐
in Britain
• Cottages, farms, apartments and chalets
• Over 400 places to stay
• Pet-Friendly accommodation

Short Break Holidays ☐
in Britain
• Accommodation for holidays and weekends away

Tick your choice above and send your order and payment to

**FHG Guides Ltd. Abbey Mill Business Centre
Seedhill, Paisley, Scotland PA1 1TJ
TEL: 0141- 887 0428 • FAX: 0141- 889 7204
e-mail: admin@fhguides.co.uk**

Deduct 10% for 2/3 titles or copies; 20% for 4 or more.

Send to: NAME ....

             ADDRESS ....

             ....

             ....

             POST CODE ....

I enclose Cheque/Postal Order for £ ....

             SIGNATURE ....DATE ....

Please complete the following to help us improve the service we provide.
How did you find out about our guides?:

☐ Press   ☐ Magazines   ☐ TV/Radio   ☐ Family/Friend   ☐ Other